Israel and Settler Society

Israel and
Settler Society

Lorenzo Veracini

Pluto Press
LONDON • ANN ARBOR, MI

First published 2006 by Pluto Press
345 Archway Road, London N6 5AA
and 839 Greene Street, Ann Arbor, MI 48106

www.plutobooks.com

British Library Cataloguing in Publication Data
A catalogue record for this book is available from the British Library

ISBN   0 7453 2501 7 hardback
ISBN   0 7453 2500 9 paperback

Library of Congress Cataloging-in-Publication Data applied for

10   9   8   7   6   5   4   3   2   1

Designed and produced for Pluto Press by
Chase Publishing Services Ltd, Fortescue, Sidmouth, EX10 9QG, England
Typeset from disk by Stanford DTP Services, Northampton, England
Printed and bound in the European Union by
Antony Rowe Ltd, Chippenham and Eastbourne, England

Contents

1   Introduction: Comparing Colonial Conditions   1

2   The Geography of Unilateral Separation:
    On Israeli Apartheids   16
    Comparing Colonial Settler Projects   18
    The Bantustanization of Palestinian Space   25
    The Racialization of Palestinian Mobility   31

3   The Troubles of Decolonization:
    France/Algeria, Israel/Palestine   41
    Comparing Wars of Decolonization   43
    Winning the Wars of Decolonization   50
    Narratives of the Wars of Decolonization   57

4   Founding Violence and Settler Societies:
    Rewriting History in Israel and Australia   64
    The 'New' Israeli History   68
    Australian History and Aboriginal History   74
    History Writing and Deadlocked Reconciliations   78

5   Conclusion: Imperial Engagements and the
    Negotiation of Israel and Palestine   87

Notes   97
Bibliography   135
Index   149

1
Introduction: Comparing Colonial Conditions

This book challenges two paradigmatic aspects of a wide historical literature: first, that the Israeli–Palestinian struggle is intractably unique and largely defies comparative approaches (Israel and Palestine are cited here in alphabetical order), and, second, that this struggle consists exclusively or mainly of a conflict of national/religious revival/liberation and bears little resemblance with typically colonial conflicts.

On the contrary, *Israel and Settler Society* approaches this conflict by utilizing a colonial framework of interpretation and a number of comparative test cases. Specifically, it develops the notion that the current circumstances of Israel/Palestine are determined by colonial conditions and a settler colonial system of institutional and personal relationships.[1] Colonial circumstances could be broadly defined as an association of both elements contained in David Fieldhouse's classic analytical distinction between 'colonization' and 'colonialism'.[2] Fieldhouse presented colonization as the successful reproduction of a European society in a colonial context, a dynamic clearly associated with the visceral metaphor embedded in the etymology of the term. 'Colonialism', on the other hand, is understood as the successful imposition of political and economic control over a colonial domain. Conversely, a viable definition of a settler

1

society could depart from Anthony Smith's 1986 authoritative description of a settler state, with its emphasis on a progressive narrative of original indigenous dispossession followed by multicultural inclusion. *Israel and Settler Society* contends that the historical experience of Zionist development in Israel/Palestine meets both these definitions.

While this notion is hardly breaking new ground and the colonialist nature of Zionism as an historical enterprise is frequently mentioned – Baruch Kimmerling, for example, published *Zionism and Territory* in 1983, and one should also mention Gershon Shafir's *Land, Labor, and the Origins of the Israeli-Palestinian Conflict*, which regarded Zionism as a form of 'European overseas expansion in a frontier region' – the paradigm with which the conflict is generally framed tends to discount the colonial genealogy and current phenomenology of the confrontation by foregrounding religious and nationalist features. As a result, the current colonial dimension of the conflict is not often examined in detail.

Many contributions refer to the fact that historical Zionism is essentially a colonial enterprise, albeit a unique one (yet again, as a comparative historian of colonialism, I cannot recall a colonial historiography that does not stress the stubborn uniqueness of its historical experience), and some of the debates over the 'new' Israeli historiography in the 1990s involved a discussion of the colonial elements of Zionist settlement.[5] Kimmerling has called for a comparative approach involving an analysis of settlement processes in North and South America, South Africa, Algeria, Australia and New Zealand in order to 'deal with Israel's colonial legacy, the very allusion to which is taboo, in both Israeli society and Israeli historiography', and Anita Shapira admitted that 'defining a movement as settlement-colonialism may well help to clarify the relations between the settling nation and the native one'; yet, this call and this acknowledgement have not been extensively pursued.[6] Even when the colonial origins of the conflict are revealed, the articulation of the dynamics that transformed a typically

Peter. The end of colonization is the conflict of opposing nationalisms,

colonial context into an intractable conflict of opposing nationalisms is rarely explored.[7] And if the current colonial dimension of the conflict is sometimes mentioned but not as often pursued, the same could be said with regards to a comparative methodology, frequently approached yet rarely the subject of more extensive research.[8]

Although it focuses on Israel as a settler society, by emphasizing a colonial circumstance, *Israel and Settler Society* ultimately responds to what has become a pressing need to interpret Palestinian agency. There is a recurring and entrenched incapacity in otherwise subtle and highly informed analyses of the conflict to assess the rationale that informs some of the choices of the Palestinian resistance. I contend that a systematic disregard of the colonially determined characteristics of the Palestinian struggle contributes to a specific interpretative deficiency.

abnormal / unreliability of the Palestinian struggle (colonially)

Israeli daily *Haaretz* analyst Yoel Marcus has brilliantly expressed this in an October 2004 piece entitled 'Get down from the roof you crazies'. The background of Marcus's piece is an escalation in the launch of Qassam rockets from the northern sector of the Gaza Strip (Qassam rockets are almost homemade projectiles Palestinian militants shoot towards Israeli territory; however, their restricted range and low efficacy have improved with time); this escalation triggered the longest and deadliest offensive of the Israeli Defense Force (IDF) in Gaza. His article exemplifies an apparent interpretative impasse:

> Now is the time to repeat the immortal words of Israel's former finance minister, Yigal Horowitz, for the benefit of the Palestinians: 'Get down from the roof, you crazies!' What is the matter with these people? Why, every time the door opens a crack for some Israeli compromise or concession, do they suddenly have this urge to maim and kill?
>
> Why, after the Oslo Accords, which Israel went through hell and high water to approve, did they unleash a campaign of bloody terror, blowing up buses, shopping malls, cafes, restaurants and markets? Why did they go on an indiscriminate murder spree,

butchering citizens of all ages? Why did they launch another wave of terror at the split second that another opportunity arose for a settlement brokered by President Clinton at Camp David? Why is every senior American peacemaker sent here to tie up the loose ends of some deal always greeted by a terror attack that sabotages the mission even before it begins?

None of this is any clearer today. Why, when the patriarch of the settlements decides in his old age to disengage from Gaza – when he makes up his mind to clear out all inhabitants, businesses and military posts, and on top of that, evacuate four West Bank settlements to get the ball rolling – have the Palestinians gone on a rampage? Why are they attacking, ambushing, and wildly shooting Qassam rockets at Sderot? I say Palestinians, and not Hamas, because the Palestinian Authority has more power and say-so than we think. If the PA didn't want Sderot bombarded, it wouldn't be.[9]

Besides the debatable validity of some of its assumptions, the most striking feature of this approach seems to be a failure in detecting a rational agency informing Palestinian actions. Classic reflections on the nature of colonial circumstances can be of help. While Marcus does not appear to be interested in addressing an apparent and self-confessed interpretative gap, his posture resonates in many ways with the 'opaqueness' of the colonized as it was identified by Albert Memmi in *The Colonizer and the Colonized* (1957):

> The humanity of the colonized, rejected by the colonizer, becomes opaque. It is useless, he asserts, to try to forecast the colonized's actions ('They are unpredictable!' 'With them, you never know!'). It seems to him that strange and disturbing impulsiveness controls the colonized. The colonized must indeed be very strange, if he remains so mysterious after years of living with the colonizer.[10]

Framed in this light, Marcus's rhetorical questions confirm a typically colonial state of mind:

> What is the point of all this violence in the Gaza Strip? The accepted theory is that Hamas wants to take credit for expelling Israel, which it needs for internal political purposes. But Hamas doesn't need to kill women and children now that the prime minister has decided on his own to pull out of Gaza. Everyone knows Israel

is taking the first step because it hasn't been able to eradicate terror by force. Israel withdrew unilaterally and unconditionally from Lebanon for the same reason. So Hamas and the Palestinian Authority can boast just as well about kicking us out of Gaza without starting a new cycle of bloodshed.

With all due respect for the Palestinians' right to an independent state, there's a screw loose somewhere. Colin Powell was right on the ball when he said the intifada has done nothing for the Palestinian cause and the time has come to call it quits. But the Palestinians never caught on. They know nothing about the workings of democratic procedure in Israel. They don't get it. They don't understand that the process of leaving Gaza, like the process of implementing the Oslo Accords, requires national consensus, a government decision, a parliamentary majority – all of which take time.

Another thing they don't get is that their impatience and embrace of violence have turned the tables politically in this country. Peaceniks have gone over to the far right. Every time public opinion tilts in the direction of concession and compromise – for example, the overwhelming majority in favor of Sharon's disengagement plan – the Palestinians do something that ends up helping the opponents of evacuation ... But as Abba Eban liked to say, the Palestinians never miss an opportunity to miss an opportunity ....[11]

Yes: why? I contend that there is as well a flaw somewhere in the lens through which Palestinian agency is generally interpreted. *Israel and Settler Society* sets out to address Marcus's questions to some extent, but intends to focus as well on the origins and character of what amounts to a generalized interpretative deficiency. In the end, Marcus also did not get it: he did not get that disengagement without some degree of decolonization will be impracticable and, in fact, will not even constitute disengagement. Most importantly, while he ultimately does not respect a Palestinian right to an independent state, he also doesn't perceive that an understanding of the Palestinian struggle cannot be limited to an appraisal of the outcomes of a struggle for statehood and therefore cannot be judged on that merit.

On the other hand, Frantz Fanon noted in the 1950s that
'the natives' challenge to the colonial world is not a rational
confrontation of points of view'.[12] The point, of course, is
not whether his rhetoric celebration of anti-colonial violence
is appropriate – it is not – rather, it is a matter of measuring
whether the dynamics he detected and described can be used
in the comprehension of the current conditions of Israel/
Palestine. Besides, Marcus's piece also shows that some Israeli
commentators very rarely miss an opportunity to refer to Abba
Eban's remark that Palestinians never miss an opportunity to
miss an opportunity.

As regards Marcus's questions, Jean-Paul Sartre's 1961
exhortation to read Fanon may provide a contributing point:
'Read Fanon: you will know that, in their time of powerlessness,
murderous madness is the collective unconscious of the
colonized.'[13] But to read Fanon in this context one should be
able and willing to first recognize the current colonial dimension
of Israel/Palestine.[14] This is its main purpose: *Israel and Settler
Society* is a contribution to detecting the reproduction of
coloniality in Israel/Palestine during the 1990s and in more
recent years. (*Israel and Settler Society* also suggests reading
Sartre's work on 1950s France and the colonial question: you
will know that a settler polity facing an incessant erosion
of its democratic life in the face of securitarian discourses
and paranoias must coherently and honestly face the issue of
colonialism and all its consequences.[15])

Indeed, typical markers of a colonial condition can be
detected in many aspects of the current confrontation. Israeli
difficulties in negotiating with a Palestinian counterpart
are indicative of something more multifaceted than the
mere necessity of retaining dominion over an ideologically
charged country and fulfil the project of a religiously and
ethnically homogeneous settler state. Besides colonial warfare,
coordination with an Indigenous other was always within the
cultural horizon of colonialism. On the other hand, negotiation
requires an initial degree of decolonization. Israeli negotiator

Daniel Levy detected a distinctive colonial state of mind when he commented on Ariel Sharon's discomfort in dealing with an autonomous Palestinian political dynamic:

> Perhaps Sharon feels at home with only two types of Arabs: those who can be demonized as the enemy and those who can be co-opted as collaborators. Yasser Arafat could easily be depicted as the former [yet he had been visualized as the latter during the years of Oslo]. Mustafa Dudin, from Dura near Hebron, who was leader of the Village Leagues in the early 1980s – which then-defense minister Sharon created to implement his limited autonomy-without-territory plan – is an example of the 'good Arab'.[16]

Moreover, the incapacity to commit to a specific timetable for the relinquishment of control is also very much part of a colonial mentality. Permanent withdrawal from, or relinquishment of control of, a specific area would be impossible without abandoning an interpretation of history that views 'progress' in terms of Palestinian erasure/absence. As I will suggest, this vision of history (and of Israel), a vision that measures its development as a function of Palestinian dispossession, cannot accept – in the present, or in a historicized future – that Palestinians may be entitled to sovereign rights. A Palestinian polity that is more than a Bantustan, or that is not a transitory accommodation or an interim agreement, would epitomize the end of a specific and deeply entrenched settler narrative.[17]

Perhaps it is not a coincidence that an enhanced degree of attention has focused especially on the psychological outcomes of the implementation of the Gaza disengagement plan.[18] In this case, the obvious trauma of withdrawing and abandoning settlers' homes is also compounded with a collective trauma associated with the process of tearing apart important tenets of a typically colonialist set of mind.

When, in January 2000, Israeli Prime Minister Ehud Barak appeared to offer a maximalist version of an 'autonomy without independence' blueprint (a series of separated entities that were to be as extended as far as possible without losing their constituent character) the Israeli colonial mind had reached the limit of its negotiating agenda: anything more would have required a decolonization of the Israeli–Palestinian relationship.[19] The myths surrounding the 'generous offer' of Prime Minister Barak fail to detect the intrinsically colonial character of his negotiating platform. Two narratives of that summit have by now emerged: that the Palestinian leadership failed to accept a generous offer or, conversely, that the Palestinian party could not accept what they were offered.[20] While the establishment of a more balanced counter-narrative is a positive development, both these interpretations may need to be integrated by a third one, in which the Camp David summit had become a negotiating anticlimax, when the Israeli side ended up not offering a deal that could be maintained. It was a convergence of realistic approaches: nothing unfeasible was proposed (or accepted) during the summit. And, alas, what was not proposed could not be rejected. Rather than accepting the existence of an autonomous Palestinian polity and its effective sovereignty, the Israeli establishment preferred – with a bipartisan decision – to progressively unfold the Oslo 'peace' process. Any undefeated colonial power would most probably act in a similar way.

Colonial tropes can be detected in many of the stories coming out of Israel/Palestine. Tali Fahima's administrative detention (arrest without trial – the first Israeli woman to be subjected to it) in late 2004 is one such episode. A Jewish Israeli woman going to live with a Palestinian wanted man in the Jenin refugee camp of all places, and acting outside the boundaries of established and recognizable political practice ('a right-winger all her life', she acted alone and did not belong to any organization) inevitably crosses a number of colonially determined red lines and is bound to raise anxieties that are typical of a colonial consciousness. Her actions posed a threat that, while very different from the security concerns that were mentioned in order to create her terrorist image, is, none the less, especially destabilizing. This may contribute to explaining the reasons why, despite the fact that all the accusations relating to her alleged involvement in terrorist activity proved to be unsubstantiated, the Israeli establishment decided to insist with her detention.[21]

Reactions to the assassination of Israeli Minister for Tourism Rehavam Zeevi epitomize another such moment. While his assassination specifically challenged the invulnerability of a colonial regime – an invulnerability that is traditionally expressed through the untouchability of its political personnel – an angry insistence on the apprehension of his killers had become a marker of the necessity of sustaining a colonial boundary perceived as weakening. Paradoxically, this was happening in the context of daily bloodshed; a killing, however, that only involved undifferentiated Palestinians, Israeli settlers, soldiers and civilians, and did not involve a raw nerve of a colonial lifestyle consciousness.[22] There is a telling difference between reactions to Prime Minister Yitzhak Rabin's assassination and Zeevi's. It is a difference that typically resonates with a classic colonial scenario: for the white man that hits a white man is guaranteed a trial; conversely, hell must be brought upon the slave that hits his master.

If it is true, as historian Zeev Sternhell has highlighted, that Rabin's assassination is the only example of a political assassination in a democratic regime that entirely fulfils its objectives, it is also true that Zeevi's elimination was also a 'targeted assassination' and a crucial moment in an attempt to dismantle a colonial circumstance by introducing an element of reciprocity.[23] The growing mythology of the 'battle for Jenin' – 'Jeningrad', as Yasser Arafat called it – is also part of a similar process: for once, the resistance of armed Palestinians, although militarily doomed, was directly challenging the Israeli army. In a colonial context, military effectiveness is not always the main point; this kind of reciprocity is rarely good news for a colonial power.

The racializing effect of a specific and emerging version of ethnocratic Zionism is a topic that is rarely mentioned, and even less researched is its psychological effectiveness.[24] From the analysis of this conflict emerges an attention to an 'accounting' of casualties and a focus on the corporality of 'the other' that can only be understood in the context of a colonial struggle and relationship. How to explain the irresistible temptation to 'mark' the body of Palestinian militants? It is a macabre concept. In November 2004 the Israeli daily *Yedioth Ahronoth* published extensive photographic evidence of practices of bodily mutilation of Palestinian militants and civilians carried out by elite units of the Army. These images included pictures representing soldiers posing with body parts of Palestinian casualties, sticking a decapitated head on an iron rod with a cigarette, etc.[25] According to testimonies collected by the Breaking the Silence organization and released in January 2005, a military doctor gave lessons in anatomy using the body of a Palestinian casualty:

> ... the 'lesson' had taken place following a clash between an armed Palestinian and an IDF force. The soldier said that the Palestinian's body had been riddled with bullets and that some of his internal organs had spilled out. The doctor pronounced the man dead and then 'took out a knife and began to cut off parts of the body', the soldier said. 'He explained the various parts to us – the membrane that covers the lungs, the layers of the skin, the liver, stuff like that.'[26]

On the other hand, after a successful attack against Israeli soldiers in Gaza in May 2004, body parts of the fallen soldiers were paraded by a number of militant groups and kept for a few days until it was agreed that they should be returned to Israeli hands.[27]

How to account as well for the unshakeable support for the indiscriminate killing of civilians displayed by the Palestinian public opinion during the Second Intifada? One of the differences between the First and the Second Intifadas may lie in the transition from a challenge against an occupying power to a challenge against Zionism's 'iron wall', a barrier made explicit especially by the colonizer's bodily untouchability. Of course, these transformations should be contextualized in relation to the 'native policy' that Israel has developed in the Occupied Territories during the 1990s (that is, Bantustanization plus a doubling of the settler population) and to its conversion from an occupying power to a segregationist regime. The attempt to establish/consolidate a specific version of colonial regime informs the typology and outward appearances of this conflict. In this way, a revolutionary struggle of national liberation was transformed in a fight that had to be expressed also and especially in terms of anti-colonial rebellion.[28]

Fanon insisted that the true enemy of the colonized is the European settler: in Africa, it was in the settler colonies – in Algeria, but also in Kenya, Southern Rhodesia, and Angola and Mozambique – that decolonization had become an especially brutal process.[29] Israel/Palestine in the years of the Second Intifada resonates dangerously with this logic. Edward Said, among others, insisted authoritatively on the genius of Fanon's work, on its capacity to encapsulate the intimate nature of the relationship between colonizer and colonized:

The Wretched of the Earth is a hybrid work – part essay, part imaginative story, part philosophical analysis, part psychological case history, part nationalist allegory, part visionary transcendence of history. It begins with a territorial sketch of the colonial space, separated into the clean, well-lighted European city and the dark, fetid, ill-lit casbah. From this Manichean and physically grounded stalemate Fanon's entire work follows, set in motion, so to speak, by the native's violence, a force intended to bridge the gap between white and non-white. For Fanon violence, as I said earlier, is the synthesis that overcomes the reification of white man as subject, Black man as object. [This is a section where Said recognizes in Fanon Georg Lukacs's unorthodox Marxism] This, he [Lukacs, but also Fanon] says, could be overcome by an act of mental will, by which one lonely mind could join another by imagining the common bond between them, breaking the enforced rigidity that kept human beings as slaves to tyrannical outside forces. Hence reconciliation and synthesis between subject and object.

Fanon's violence, by which the native overcomes the division between whites and natives, corresponds very closely to Lukacs's thesis about overcoming fragmentation by an act of will; Lukacs calls this 'no single, unrepeatable tearing of the veil that masks the process but the unbroken alternation of ossification, contradiction and movement'. Thus the subject-object reification in its prison-like immobility is destroyed.[30]

The disappearance of a postcolonial horizon, despite the internationally sanctioned dealings of Madrid, Oslo and Wye River Plantation, constituted a crucial turning-point. At a time in which the possibility of disengaging from Israel's colonial oppression became postponed into an indefinite future, a colonial phenomenology began increasingly to inform relationships. On the subject of extra-judicial executions, a widespread practice in the Israeli anti-insurgency approach, Lisa Hajjar concluded that Italian philosopher Giorgio Agamben's influential notion of *homo sacer* (a person devoid of citizenship or political rights and reduced to the state of naked life; a person that can be killed without it being considered a crime) can be applied to Palestinian resisters.[31]

At this specific intersection, an inversion becomes apparent: as it would seem appropriate in a colonial circumstance, the colonized becomes expendable, and – interiorizing his/her domination – knows him/her as such. It should be noted that the control of the body has always been one major obsession of the colonial mind, a fixation engendered by the recognition of colonialism's outer limit. The Palestinians that annihilate themselves in order to kill must face a condition in which a suicidal determination has become an ontologically available one.[32] Obviously, Israel's colonial project would prefer this process to go no further than the metaphorical level. This phenomenon, however, largely escapes colonial surveillance;

the quietness of a colonial relationship is upset, and its pretence
of normality is turned upside down.

The fundamental importance of the Israeli–Palestinian conflict
in an international context has been extensively highlighted,
uniting commentators that would otherwise agree on very little.
Left-wing French intellectual Etienne Balibar and American
Zionist Christian and television evangelist Pat Robertson (but
these are definitely random examples) interpret this dispute as
a crucial moment in the articulation of international agendas.[33]
However, despite this perceived centrality, there still is a
painful need to investigate a number of features that inform
this conflict. Approaching the Israeli–Palestinian dispute and
its dynamics without an informed perception of its colonial
character can be frustrating. To read, for example, a football
game one needs to refer to its code(s); that is how I ended up
writing this book. Besides, in an era of pre-emptive surgical
strikes, it is perhaps wise to suggest the homeopathic principle
that *similia similibus*, that is, that similarity and comparisons
are one way to a cure.[34]

Israel and Settler Society compares Israel/Palestine with three
locations of a settler-determined colonial expansion and focuses
thematically on segregation, mobility restriction, racialization,
histiography, narrative and discourses around resistance
and repression. Chapters 2 and 3 discuss the repression of
Palestinian resistances; Chapter 4 addresses historiography
and the politics of history. In its conclusion, *Israel and Settler
Society* also proposes to integrate interpretations of US policy
regarding Israel/Palestine with an analysis mindful of two
intertwined colonial imaginations.

Chapter 2 appraises the increasing occurrence of references to
apartheid in relation to Israel/Palestine and assesses a developing
practice of exclusion through a comparison with South Africa's
policies during the apartheid era. The first section of this chapter
constitutes an outline for a comparative approach; the second

and conclusive sections of the chapter interpret the current phase of the conflict and contribute to a growing comparative investigation of two colonial circumstances.

Chapter 3 proposes a comparative analysis of two conflicts in which a settler project supported by a colonial power reluctant to relinquish control over an area deemed strategically and ideologically essential was and is opposed to a nationalist movement struggling for independence. The chapter examines Israeli responses to the Second Intifada by comparing them with the repressive strategies developed by the Fourth French Republic to deal with the Algerian war of decolonization. In this context, a reading of the French war in Algeria and the ways in which it influenced the transition to the Fifth French Republic can shed light on the current confrontation in the West Bank and Gaza and on current institutional impasses and debates in Israel.

Chapter 4 addresses the evolution of history writing and debates in two very different contexts: Israel and Australia. It highlights a set of shared features in the politics of history and in public discourse. Two themes emerge as central to each historiography and its evolution: the final acknowledgement of the dispossession of the original inhabitants, and the defective legitimacy of the institutions of the state until a settlement with the dispossessed is reached. Characteristic of both circumstances is the obvious difficulty of coming to terms with a history epitomized by extreme violence and denial, and a deadlock in the reconciliation processes.

Israel and Settler Society does not present cross-cultural research. This work mainly relies on Israeli sources because its subject matter is Israel *as a settler society* and Zionism as a settler project. While it suggests that analyses of Palestinian agency should be aware of a colonial dimension, it focuses on Israel and on the ways colonialism shapes its circumstances.

Research presented in Chapters 2 and 3 appeared in contributions published by *Arena Journal*; an earlier version of Chapter 4 originally appeared in *Australian Historical Studies*: I thank the editors of these publications for granting permission to use this material in the writing of this book. I also need to especially thank John Docker, Ann Curthoys and Tim Rowse from Canberra, Mark Finnane and David Carter from Brisbane, and the Australian Studies Centre at the University of Queensland. Their support had become essential when I was writing on settler societies and conducting a somewhat unsettled life. I also need to thank *Haaretz*, Italian daily *il manifesto*, and their free Internet service. Without the latter and the daily immersion in the story of the world it provides, this planet would feel much less like home.

2
The Geography of Unilateral Separation: on Israeli Apartheids

A rising in a variety of contexts in recent years, 'apartheid' has become a common reference point in analyses of developments in Israel/Palestine.[1] The World Conference Against Racism in Durban, South Africa, in September 2001 and the deliberations of the International Court of Justice in The Hague in March 2004 are two important passages in a comprehensive process.[2] In fact, a section of the Palestinian national movement has developed a strategy aimed at isolating Israel internationally on this basis.[3] On the other hand, an awareness of the growing relevance of this issue was mentioned, for example, in a report prepared by the Israeli Foreign Ministry in August 2004. This document prepared by the Center for Political Research warned that the country's standing could deteriorate and end up resembling apartheid-era South Africa's.[4] The concept of apartheid has entered Israeli public consciousness and has been put on the political agenda.[5]

These developments are consistent with one of the last contributions of Edward Said. While reflecting (rather pessimistically) on the options open to the Palestinian national movement, he highlighted both the absolute need for a comprehensive change in leadership – one of his long-standing demands – and a far-reaching change in strategy. Quoting Nelson Mandela, he specifically advocated a struggle capable of affecting 'the imagination and dreams of the entire world', a struggle capable of offering 'the whole society – even the Whites who apparently benefited from the Apartheid – the only way that enable[ed] the preservation of basic human values'.[6] Said referred to the struggles of black South Africans and how they had ultimately received the support of US public opinion: 'Uninformed and yet open to appeals for justice as they are, Americans are capable of reacting as they did to the ANC campaign against apartheid, which finally changed the balance of forces inside South Africa.'[7]

Indeed, although Palestinian and some Israeli observers have insisted for decades on the racist and segregationist character of Israel's domination of Palestinian political life, recent developments, including the construction of the 'separation' barrier in the West Bank, have provided Palestinian commentators with further reason to advance the apartheid argument.[8] Conversely, arguments against the idea of apartheid-like Israeli policies have also appeared, but typically they tend to foreclose on the possibility of comparative analysis. For example, *The Economist* recently presented a typical refutation of the apartheid argument:

> Others revile it [Israel] as the new apartheid regime. This last accusation is inexact. Unlike blacks under apartheid, Israel's own Arabs enjoy full political rights. What is more, the Israel–Palestinian struggle looks less tractable. The South Africans had plenty of land to share, and none of it was holy. White South Africans feared expropriation, Israelis fear extinction, and the Holy Land has no Mandela.[9]

And yet, each of these observations needs qualification. As will be shown later, Palestinian Israelis do not enjoy full political rights, some black South Africans enjoyed a degree of political franchise during the apartheid era, white South Africans feared extinction as much as Israeli Jews fear expropriation, and much of Afrikaner nationalism was built around the notion of a special covenant between settler communities and God. But quite apart from these considerations, *The Economist*'s approach amounts mainly to reiterating the obvious fact that Israel/Palestine is not South Africa. On the contrary, a comparative approach aimed at testing the assertion of apartheid-like Israeli policies is interested precisely in highlighting corresponding developments in the context of obviously different circumstances. As well, *The Economist* fails to mention that the Holy Land has no Frederik W. de Klerk either.

While references to apartheid in relation to Israel/Palestine have become more frequent, a detailed comparison of the dynamics of these two colonial processes has not yet been proposed.[10] The first section of this chapter constitutes a tentative outline for a comparative approach; the second and concluding sections interpret the current phase of the confrontation in the light of this analysis.

Comparing Colonial Settler Projects

The year 1948 was a fateful one for the colonial histories of both Israel/Palestine and South Africa. Whereas the colonial project established after the Israeli victory in the War of Independence/Nakba exhibited crucial differences from the colonial circumstances established after the general election victory of the South African National Party in the same year, both colonial situations were premised on the notion of an original dispossession and an actual process of expulsion of indigenous peoples. There are other significant similarities: each power eventually became the only nuclear actor in a regional context of manifest hostility and enduring isolation, both enjoyed Western support in the context of the Cold War, and both underwent a deep reassessment of their position after its conclusion.

While a particular insistence on the colonial origins of current conflicts has recently been a shared feature of both South African and Israeli historiographies, a comparative analysis of the settler imaginations underscoring both the apartheid regime in South Africa and the evolving circumstances of Israel's settler domination of the Palestinians would highlight a shared repertoire of themes, tropes and refrains, as well as shared constructions of 'the natives' as both romantic and especially and gratuitously violent.[11] Like other settler societies, Israel and South Africa also share a particular preoccupation about demography. Despite parallel mythologies of the colonized space as an empty land, the indigenous question has been continuously raised and represented in anxious demographic terms – the fear of an increasing African or Palestinian birth rate respectively – contradicting the very notion of a depopulated space. While this is a common tendency in most settler societies, in South Africa and Israel/Palestine comparable 'high frontierity' conditions may have determined a settler imagination obsessed with needing to manipulate demography in order to ensure an 'equilibrium' acceptable for the colonizing effort.[12]

Smith's authoritative work on the 'Chosen peoples', for example, deals with Zionism and Afrikaner nationalism in the same chapter and highlights their comparable character.[13] Both Zionism and Afrikaner nationalism have insisted on indigenous absence, on a 'land without a people', or the emptiness of the South African frontier, arguing that the indigenous peoples had entered the geographic space identified by the colonizing project only at some late historical stage.[14] Contrary to the experience of other settler societies, Palestinians and black South Africans were never accorded the status of 'first nations', thus preparing the ground for establishing notions of population 'transfer', which sections of both Zionism and Afrikaner nationalism have enthusiastically supported.[15] As well, and very importantly, both Palestinians and black South Africans were denied their ethnic and national specificity, being perceived merely as local segments of a wider, more undifferentiated indigenous context (the 'Arabs', 'native Africans'). Again, this non-distinction would prove functional to notions of transfer.

On the other hand, a comparative analysis would also need to appraise very different approaches to notions of biological racism and sexism. Contrary to Afrikaner nationalism, Zionism traditionally refrained from developing explicitly racializing discourses and has been relatively more attentive to the inclusion of women in a specific settler ethos, including its political and military personnel. However, it may be argued that these characteristics of an Israeli and Zionist settler ethos have been progressively eroded with the growth of neo-Zionist and fundamentalist tendencies in Israeli society during the 1980s and 1990s.[16]

More importantly, as highlighted, for example, by Leila Farsakh in her comparative analysis, a significant difference in colonial practice is apparent in South Africa's reliance on an Indigenous labour force as compared to Zionist attempts to prevent dependence on Palestinian labour. The difference is striking: 75 per cent of the total South African labour force was indigenous, compared to only 15 per cent of the Jewish sector of the Israeli economy between 1948 and 1967.[17] Generally speaking, apartheid was established in South Africa to deal with a situation in which the colonial project needed both the land and the workforce. Institutionalized residential and territorial discrimination was functional to a situation in which people were allowed to work but not to reside in the same place. Such a situation was not present in Israel before 1967, where the colonial project seemed to need the land but not its people.

Farsakh stresses how that fundamental premise of Zionist colonialism was reversed in 1967 and how it was with the victory over the Arab armies and the occupation of Gaza and the West Bank in that year that the colonial circumstances of apartheid South Africa and Israel/Palestine began to converge significantly:

> After the 1967 war Israel consolidated its claims to the occupied land. The rightwing government elected in 1977 developed an elaborate policy of territorial integration and demographic separation. The military government in the West Bank and Gaza Strip (WBGS) expropriated and enclosed Palestinian land and allowed the transfer of Israeli settlers to the occupied territories: they continued to be governed by Israeli laws. The government also enacted different military laws and decrees to regulate the civilian, economic and legal affairs of Palestinian inhabitants. These strangled the Palestinian economy and increased its dependence and integration into Israel. From 1967–90 the borders between Israel and the occupied territories were kept open. More than a third of the Palestinian labour force was employed in Israel and generated over a quarter of the territories' GDP.[18]

While this chronology is consistent with the views of important sectors of Israeli opinion, others have highlighted the continuity of Zionist settlement activities before and after this juncture.[19] Yet, historically, Zionist colonial labour policies have oscillated dramatically. According to Shafir's analysis, during the first and second Aliyas (Jewish migration to Palestine; 1882–1903 and 1904–14), no less than six different models of colonial relations were elaborated vis-à-vis the Palestinian presence and in relation to the question of whether the developing colonial economy should rely on Palestinian labour.[20] Only at a later stage, after the conversion to the struggle for the 'conquest of labour', did Zionism become an exclusivist colonial settler movement. After 1967, supremacist approaches as to which model of colonial relations should be imposed on the Palestinians resurfaced (quite significantly, white South African labour organizations had also faced a similar dilemma and also expressed a South African version of the 'conquest of labour').[21]

None the less, with regards to an Israeli determination of controlling a large Palestinian population, 1967 was much less of a turning-point. After this date, Israel demanded the land and, without enacting a population transfer, its peoples as well. Whatever the differences and similarities between South Africa and Israel at this level, there is an important parallel between the two contexts in relation to the long-term effects of the Israeli occupation of the Palestinian Territories, with the Israeli economy having exclusive access to a large 'captive market', including the possibilities for capital and fiscal extraction that have accompanied the occupation.[22] At the same time, reliance on a native workforce is less of a discriminating point between the two colonial contexts if we consider that, besides a labour-intensive mining and industrial economy that demanded cheap access to a large native workforce, a parallel South African settler model of land control had also historically developed in a way that dispensed to a large extent with indigenous labour.[23] In the end, Cecil Rhodes's 'I prefer land to niggers' could apply to a Zionist attitude to land and Arabs.[24]

One significant difficulty in effectively comparing the two conditions is represented by the different regimes under which Palestinian Israelis and Palestinians of the Occupied Territories are living.[25] Farsakh, for example, acknowledges this distinction:

> The first issue is the geographical delineation of Israeli 'apartheid': does it cover all of Israel or only the WBGS? Palestinians living beyond the Green Line are Israeli citizens, while Palestinians in the WBGS are not. The former are not confined to specific geographic areas out of which they cannot move, nor are they excluded from the Israeli political process – they vote and can be elected, though they are discriminated against. The latter are an occupied population awaiting a political solution.[26]

But the position of Palestinian Israelis is also changing dramatically, and the events of October 2000, for example, when the distinction between Palestinian Israelis and Palestinians of the Occupied Territories was disregarded by the repressive instruments of the Israeli state, are indicative of an apparent deterioration of relations. Other developments are consistent with this evolution, including a growing feeling of political disenfranchisement among Palestinian Israelis.[27] In fact, Palestinian Israelis are also awaiting a political solution.

As well, and in a comparative perspective, one should also consider that some degree of political representation was accorded to some black South Africans under apartheid, and that the federal organization of apartheid South Africa determined a variety of administrative statuses for non-white citizens, including limited access to some political and personal freedoms. Ultimately, the administrative lines dividing the subjects of the apartheid regime had also distinguished between different groups, their location, and their degree of interaction with the institution of the state.

The prospect of a territorial partition has been noted as one major difference between the two colonial contexts. However, partition was also proposed by sections of the Afrikaner opinion as a possible solution to the conflict in South Africa. At the same time, a reversal of the territorial integration of the West Bank and Israel proper has progressively become less and less feasible, and the possibility of meaningful partition has also faded. Both Israeli and Palestinian observers are expressing concern regarding territorial separation after the decade-long building spree of settlements that followed Oslo and have started thinking again about the possibility of a bi-national state.[28] The African National Congress was able to reject separatist positions, while the Palestinian mainstream position eventually shifted from proposing a binational state to supporting partition. Paradoxically, the two-state solution envisaged by the Oslo process was accepted by the Palestinian leadership in the context of a framework that postponed partition indefinitely while allowing for the conditions of any such division to be gradually and irreversibly removed.[29]

However, differences between South Africa and Israel/ Palestine regarding the attitude and influence of the international

community can be overemphasized. It was ultimately US
policy that largely determined the timing and outcome of the
conflict in South Africa, just as it was US power that shaped
the Oslo process, and supervised its demise.[30] In the logic of
the Cold War, a degree of support for apartheid South Africa
as a perceived bulwark against Communism was never denied,
and it was only in post-Cold War conditions that a serious
negotiation could begin to bring a very inefficient system of
political control to an end. Such a shift did not occur in the
case of Israel/Palestine during the 1990s, despite some parallels
in Bill Clinton's rhetoric regarding the Oslo process, and this
was even less so after the failure of the Camp David summit
of 2000 and, later, after the commencement of the 'War on
Terror'. This dependence on political shifts in the United States
brings us back to Said's original intuition: the only way out for
the Palestinians is to promote a 'mass campaign on behalf of
Palestinian human rights, outflanking the Zionist establishment
and going straight to the American people'.[31]

The creation of a growing network of Israeli settlements
in the West Bank, Gaza and in East Jerusalem was ultimately
based on the fragmentation of Palestinian areas. This process
of destructuring was based on arguments about 'security',
resource considerations and on an ongoing, deliberate and
scientific attempt to alter Palestinian demographics. A parallel
process – of territorial integration and social disintegration –
was taking place, and the military-bureaucratic governance of
Palestinian people in the West Bank and in Gaza was an essential
element of this development. Farsakh's conclusion that these
policies could be defined as apartheid, 'even if they were never
given such a name', is consistent with a growing literature.[32]
Smith's 1986 definition of a South African trajectory to state-
making, a polity going through 'ethnic, colonial and immigrant
phases, but now [practising] an ethnic policy within a racial
colonialism', is remarkably pertinent to Israeli history.[33]

The Bantustanization of Palestinian Space

Former Italian Prime Minister Massimo D'Alema's comments during a visit to Israel reveal Sharon's thoughts on the most appropriate arrangements for a Palestinian polity in the West Bank and Gaza. Senior *Haaretz* analyst Akiva Eldar's report of a conversation regarding Sharon's inspiration for his plans regarding 'final' arrangements for a Palestinian polity in the West Bank and Gaza is particularly telling:

> According to D'Alema, Sharon explained at length that the Bantustan model was the most appropriate solution for the conflict.
>
> The defender of Israel quickly protested, 'Surely that was your personal interpretation of what Sharon said.'
>
> D'Alema didn't give in: 'No, Sir, that is not interpretation. That is a precise quotation of your prime minister.'[34]

One essential element of South African apartheid was the creation of ten separate homelands for the different 'national' groups that were said to constitute the black population of South Africa. The unilateral character of border definition and a design uniquely based on demographic and resource considerations is indeed a shared feature of the South African experience and the proposed Palestinian polity. Sharon's blueprint for the management of the Occupied Territories – and not only its inspiration – is noticeably similar to the plan for establishing protectorates in South Africa as developed in the early 1960s.

While Bantustans were unilaterally declared and no country ever recognized their independence – except, to a degree, Israel which allowed Bophutatswana to open a diplomatic office in Tel Aviv – the effective sovereignties of these entities have had some common social and political consequences: instability and coups, military interventions, overpopulation, lack of access to sustainable resources, including water, demilitarization, and, finally, as already noted, the creation of a captive market for the 'protector' country's businesses. These are features that would characterize a Palestinian polity established according to the current negotiating platforms of the Israeli right.

Besides referring directly to South African Bantustans, Sharon has often and explicitly defined his notion of a Palestinian state:

> This Palestinian state will be completely demilitarized. It will be allowed to maintain lightly armed police and internal forces to ensure civil order. Israel will continue to control all movement in and out of the Palestinian state, will command its airspace, and not allow it to form alliances with Israel's enemies.[35]

As well as other entitlements, Israel would retain control of foreign, defence, trade, and immigration policy, and any Palestinian polity would emerge merely as a subcontractor regime. Israeli interpretations of the Oslo Accords and the ways they were eventually implemented (as well as Israeli interpretations of the 'road map'), insist on security cooperation as a prerequisite for compromise, on an ongoing negotiation of Palestinian institutions and leadership, and ultimately on Israel's right to determine Palestinian politics. Although more explicit in bypassing a Palestinian negotiating input, the recent implementation of the Gaza 'disengagement' plan did not depart from this established framework. Articles 1, 2 and 3 of the section entitled 'Security Reality after the Evacuation' dealt more with the features of a prospected Palestinian 'sovereignty' than with security. International pressure did not alter the substance of the original version of the plan:

> 1. Israel will supervise and guard the external envelope of land, will maintain exclusive control in the air space of Gaza, and will continue to conduct military activities in the sea space of the Gaza Strip.
> 2. The Gaza Strip will be demilitarized and devoid of armaments, the presence of which is not in accordance with the existing agreements between the sides.
> 3. Israel reserves for itself the basic right of self-defence, including taking *preventative* steps as well as responding by

using force against threats that will emerge from the Gaza Strip. [emphasis added][36]

While continuity of the Oslo arrangements is reaffirmed throughout the document, it is also (unilaterally) stressed that the result of this implementation will be that 'there will be no basis for the claim that the Gaza Strip is occupied territory'.[37] Indeed, both the Barak and Sharon administrations have pursued similar agendas, demanding a declaration asserting the 'end' of the occupation without actually discontinuing it.[38]

Bantustans were based on a typology of territorial segregation that, while founded in previous historical processes of colonial settlement and dispossession, was reinforced by the legal activity of the apartheid regime. Some indigenous areas were envisaged as Bantustans and the unilateral process of defining their status as 'independent' polities was initiated.[39] Yet, the Bantustan 'citizenships' that were eventually enacted between 1976 and 1981 (four of the ten Bantustans that had been planned were effectively established) were inevitably based on a process of further divestment of rights and entitlements for black South Africans who lost their status as South African subjects.

However, while lack of substantial sovereignty was an essential feature of South Africa's Bantustans, legal, economic and residential discriminations were other cornerstones of apartheid. Many commentators have pointed to the apartheid-like nature of the Israeli occupation of the West Bank and Gaza during the years of the Oslo process and to the territorial integration that was a prerequisite for the 'Bantustanization' of Palestinian population clusters.[40] Indeed, the establishment of a Palestinian Authority deprived of independent military, economic, and diplomatic capacities – the transformation of a military occupation into a context where civil order and administration should be guaranteed by a subcontractor regime – is remarkably similar to the South African experience.

But it is perhaps in the actual and projected status of Palestinian Israelis that the most significant parallels between

South Africa and Israel/Palestine can be detected. Recurring proposals for the establishment of separate institutions including a parliament for Palestinian Israelis, and calls for an interdiction of immunity for Palestinian members of the Israeli parliament, including attempts to rule on their eligibility, are all indications of new limits on effective political representation. The Or Commission, established after the bloody repression of protests in Palestinian areas in Israel during October 2000, highlighted a systematic trend towards segregation and towards the establishment of a militarized system of policing for these communities. Despite the Commission's recommendations, no action was taken to redress a deteriorating relationship.

Most of all, recurring calls for the transfer of the areas of Israel most densely populated by Palestinian Israelis to a future Palestinian polity are indicative of an apartheid-like state of mind.[41] Among other legislative initiatives, there was the submission of a bill in January 2005 which proposed withdrawing the status of Arabic as an official language in Israel.[42] Recent proposals to allow residence and withdraw citizenship rights for Palestinian Israelis in the context of a comprehensive repackaging of Israeli–Palestinian relations (as discussed by the Sharon administration in early 2004) are consistent with a process of Bantustanization that involves all Palestinians. According to these formulations, the autonomy of a Palestinian polity and the transfer (how apt a term in this context) of citizenship for Palestinian Israelis, including East Jerusalem Palestinians cut off by the 'separation' barrier, are understood as intertwined processes, underscoring a comprehensive movement towards segregation.[43]

The differences in the rhetorical stance of the Israeli administration and political right regarding the participation of East Jerusalem Palestinians in the 1996 and the January 2005 elections for the Chairman of the Palestinian Authority also epitomizes a decisive shift in approaches to the relationship between residential and political rights. What in 1996 had become one contested issue, potentially raising apprehensions regarding Israeli sovereignty over East Jerusalem, in late 2004 did not stir much controversy. However, as noted by Israeli commentator Meron Benvenisti, in East Jerusalem, Palestinian participation in the electoral process of the Palestinian Authority could

> ... serve as a precedent and example for solving 'the demographic issue' and a comfortable formula for 'a Jewish and democratic state': Palestinian residents of Israel would vote for government institutions outside of Israel's sovereign borders, thus preventing the danger of Israel becoming a binational country, heaven forbid.
>
> Today, a precedent is being set in regard to several tens of thousands of people: They are being granted the right to vote by the government of Israel, though not within Israel's borders. (It is true that in this case this is being done in accordance with a demand made by the Palestinians themselves.) Tomorrow, this precedent – which, of course, has won praise from overseas and will be enthusiastically supported by the Zionist left when it reaches the Knesset – can be used and extended to areas of the West Bank, which would be annexed to Israel under Sharon's plan of cantons. In this way, land could be annexed without its residents, and Israel could still feel supremely democratic and liberal.[44]

A corresponding process of disjunction between residency and voting entitlements was one outcome of the many appeals calling for an Israeli referendum to be held over the prospected disengagement from Gaza. These calls were expressed in the language of a democratic need to establish a mandate for an important shift in policy and yet, in the midst of a hotly contested political debate, many failed to note that a referendum which would not allow participation of all those involved (that is, the Palestinian residents of Gaza) would be a perversion of generally accepted democratic standards and would clearly replicate apartheid conditions.[45] Of course, a separation between residency rights and the rights of political representation was also present in apartheid South Africa and a conservative segment of South African opinion opposed the constitutional transformation to a post-apartheid regime on the basis that changes had not been 'democratically' endorsed.

Quite naturally, many black South Africans had continued to live outside the areas that were accorded Bantustan status; only they lost the entitlements associated with South African nationality in the process. Most importantly, it should be noted that the establishment of 'independent' Bantustans was instrumental to the deterioration of the political status of *all* black South Africans. The 'separation' fence being built inside Palestinian territory on the one hand and the rhetoric of a (future) Palestinian 'state' on the other, may conceal the converging circumstances of Palestinians on both sides of the Green Line.

A 2003 provision denying Palestinian spouses of Israeli citizens the right of residence in Israel is one further development of this type. In this case, security – the necessity of preventing terrorist infiltration – is the justification for the establishment of a special administrative regime for certain citizens according to an ethnic rationale. (However, quite significantly, Palestinian collaborators are excluded from the provisions of this Act and can be granted permanent residency in Israel.)[46] This measure – further extended in early 2005, even after the prospect of an end of violence had become a reliable one – can be framed in the context of a progressive restriction of citizenship rights of all Palestinian Israelis.[47] Based on the notion of Palestinian Israelis as a demographic 'time-bomb', it strongly echoes the laws (that is, the Prohibition of Mixed Marriages Act, 1949) which prevented South Africans from legally establishing interracial families during apartheid.

While a military administration was in charge of controlling Palestinian Israelis through a system of passes, curfews and residential controls until 1966, no law explicitly discriminated between Jewish and non-Jewish citizens (numerous laws, however, accorded special privileges to individuals to whom the Law of Return applied). Recent developments can be interpreted as a trend towards a return to a pre-1966 situation in which Palestinians are perceived simply as 'alien residents' of the state of Israel. Entitlements won over decades are now being challenged by a growing inclination towards segregation, a trend detectable both in Israeli policies in the West Bank and Gaza and epitomized by the 'separation' barrier, and by ongoing debates about the presence, entitlements and role of Palestinian Israelis.

The Racialization of Palestinian Mobility

Edward Said insisted on the importance of geographical thought to a specific sense of culture and empire both generally and explicitly; he repeatedly noted an absolute gap in geographical knowledge between Israelis and Palestinians:

> ... as I have been pointing out for several years, the Palestinians themselves have until recently been mapless. They had no detailed maps of their own at Oslo; nor, unbelievably, were there any individuals on the negotiating team familiar enough with the geography of the Occupied Territories to contest decisions or to provide alternative plans.[48]

Laurence Silberstein also noted that a Zionist enterprise had traditionally utilized a geographic form of representation in order to organize the colonizing project.[49] In a context where a technology of geographical control is deployed to its full extent in order to perpetuate colonial domination, it is both indicative and ironic that the metaphor used in relation to a plan for a nominal decolonization of the Occupied Territories refers to a 'road map'.

Said systematically denounced a geography of apartheid disguised behind 'the measured discourse of peace and bilateral negotiations'.[50] With the beginning of the Second Intifada, the geography of dispossession and segregation did not change significantly. It was the measured discourse that did, and was replaced by the language of unilateral separation and by an insistence on the need to 'sear' the Palestinian consciousness and 'impress' it with recurring displays of strength.

But unilateral separation is by definition a type of Bantustanization in which neither the international community nor the indigenous counterpart are providing an input. The Republic of South Africa had unilaterally separated from the Bantustans it was establishing while claiming there was no partner for negotiation. In that context, unilateral separation was presented as a solution – one step forward – in what was perceived as an intractable conflict that was endangering the very viability of a South African settler state. Of course, Bantustans were not a solution to the problems of apartheid; rather, they were an essential feature in an integrated system of policing and governance. 'Unilateral separation' from the Palestinians would not and did not bring an end to the occupation of Gaza and the West Bank: on the contrary, unilateral separation as it is proposed in the debates regarding Israeli withdrawal from Gaza and the 'separation' barrier will only amount to a reorganization of the structures deployed for the governance of Palestinians in the Occupied Territories. The wall, however disconnected from the Green Line, is not a step in the process of border definition as some wishful-thinking interpretations would suggest; rather, it appears to be yet another feature in a complex system of domination. This arrangement has been perceptively described by Israeli academic and commentator Jeff Halper as the 'matrix of control'.[5]

This process entails a double separation and a Bantustan-like arrangement: a long-lasting process of separation of historical Palestine from neighbouring states and an equally long-lasting process of internal separation between one Jewish and a number of Palestinian demographic blocs. As Benvenisti has noted:

> The concrete control (known as 'security') of all international borders, which Israel is succeeding in retaining at the land

crossings, the Gaza airport and ... seaport, enables it to implement the internal separation.

Control of the external wrapper is essential for the Oslo strategy, because if the Palestinians control even one border crossing – and gain the ability to maintain direct relations with the outside world – the internal line of separation will become full-fledged international borders, and Israel will lose its control over the passage of people and goods. Punctuating the external system will necessitate the establishment of a vast array of physical obstacles, crossing points and custom barriers between the enclaves of the 'internal separation', and will expose the absurdity of the tortuous and non contiguous borders of the ethnic cantons on which all the ideas of the permanent settlement are based.[52]

The unilateral Gaza pullout, which ensured Israeli control of Gaza airspace, water and border crossings, did not depart from this pattern and showed how the Israeli–Palestinian conflict should be framed less in terms of territory and more in terms of control.[53]

If it is true that one can better frame the evolving situation in Israel/Palestine by referring to the history of apartheid, it is also true that one can understand South African history through a reference to Israeli policies in respect of the mobility of the Palestinian population. Bantustanization could then be conceptualized as one stage of a transfer-based type of settler colonialism, a course of action which is attempted when prophecies of white settler demographic conquest have ultimately been disqualified and when fantasies of population transfer have been abandoned.

The institutions of apartheid, as well, are strictly linked to the urban crisis that has affected both Palestinian society and black South African urban centres. The necessity of defining an urban pattern of living for the purpose of policing and controlling is a common feature of both situations. The urban policy of the apartheid state became an essential feature of the regime; in the same way, controlling the urban areas of the West Bank and Gaza has become the essential feature of the repressive policies of the Oslo Accords and, at a later stage,

dictated the reoccupation of Palestinian centres. In South
Africa, the urban crisis that had begun in the 1960s eventually
became a crisis of the whole of the apartheid regime, and the
beginning of its end.[54] The policies that Israel is following
with regards to Palestinian urban areas are dealing with an
array of similar crises, and the 'separation' fence fits well in
this logic.

1993 was a fateful year for both the colonial settler projects
of Israel/Palestine and South Africa. At a time when some of
the institutions of apartheid were discontinued in South Africa,
behind the rhetoric of the Oslo peace process, comparable
conditions were entrenched in the West Bank and Gaza. Many
of the typical phenomena of apartheid could be detected in
Israel and the Occupied Palestinian Territories during the
years preceding the failed summit at Camp David in 2000
(and after). Among these, the creation and consolidation of a
collaborationist elite, the establishment of new labour regimes,
the reproduction of racial discourse, the multiplication of
administrative borders – lines with a different meaning for
different people – and a consistent effort to manipulate the
demographic reality and to increase the subjects of the colonial
mosaic through the arrival of foreign non-Jewish workers from
South-east Asia, Eastern Europe, China and Latin America.[55]

This population economy could always be reversed. A
double suicide bombing at the Central Bus Station in Tel Aviv
in January 2003, where six illegal foreign workers were killed
and a number of them were injured, highlighted appalling
circumstances. While many could not access medical help for
fear of deportation, the campaign against their presence and
the policy of deportation after the economy began to falter as
a consequence of the Intifada was framed in explicitly racist
terms. A piece published in the Israeli daily *Maariv* commented
that the

> ... propaganda of the immigration police against the foreign
> workers is developing into a cultural, humanitarian and political

atrocity. The television broadcasts against foreigners are becoming more and more violent. The foreign workers are presented as 'people enemies'. Their humanity is transparent, non-existent. The fact that the Israelis 'imported them' and are taking advantage of them is being denied. The propaganda incites the unemployed to act against the foreign worker. The propaganda presents those who employ foreign workers as 'traitors'. If you insert the word 'Jew' instead of 'foreign worker' in this propaganda – you will get anti-Semitism.[56]

And, as it could be expected in a colonial situation, the deterioration of the condition of illegal foreign workers became instrumental to the weakening of Palestinian circumstances: many have expressed fears that the deportation of migrant workers will end up preparing the ground and legitimizing the deportation of Palestinians.[57]

An analysis of the economic landscape confirms this pattern. While the economies of the West Bank and especially Gaza were underdeveloped and isolated from each other during the Oslo years, this course was further reinforced after the reoccupation that followed Operation Defensive Shield in April 2002. More than ever before, the Palestinian economy is now dependent on the possibility of workers entering Israel to work. As a result, South African apartheid-like conditions are being reproduced in a surprisingly similar fashion.

Quite interestingly, the 'disengagement' plan originally proposed by Sharon and successively endorsed by the US administration, detailed the way in which the current conditions of the Erez industrial zone will be maintained and possibly reproduced in another industrial area that was to be established at the southern end of the Gaza Strip.[58] The prospect of organizing industrial areas for cheap (Palestinian) labour and lucrative (Israeli) opportunities is one extraordinarily resilient aspect of an evolving situation and has characterized the years of Oslo, the reoccupation of Palestinian cities, Israeli left- and right-wing administrations, coordination with the Palestinian Authority, unilateral Israeli decision-making, the first period of the Second Intifada, and the building of the 'separation' fence. Israeli journalist Meron Rapoport has documented how some acts of land confiscation are functional to the project of transforming Palestinian peasants into an industrial workforce.[59] One reason why the military organizations of the Palestinian resistance concentrated on the Erez crossing (four suicide attacks in the first four months of 2004) may have to do more with the will to attack a symbol of the apartheid-like conditions of the Gaza Strip than military considerations.[60] After all, this is the site where the captive conditions of the Palestinian labour market is most apparent.

Israeli novelist Yitzhak Laor has commented on a widespread and ongoing drive towards the racialization of 'the Palestinians'. He quoted then Israeli Chief of Staff, Lieutenant General Moshe Yaalon:

> When I look at the overall map what disturbs me especially is the Palestinian threat and the possibility that a hostile state will acquire nuclear capability ... We have good answers for all the other threats. We have a good answer for what Hezbollah can do and for what the Syrians can do. We also have a good answer for what the Iraqis are liable to do ... The Palestinian threat is invisible, like cancer. When you are attacked externally, you see the attack, you are wounded. Cancer, on the other hand, is something internal. Therefore, I find it more disturbing, because here the diagnosis is critical. If the diagnosis is wrong and people say it's not cancer but a headache, then the response is irrelevant. But I maintain that it is cancer. My professional diagnosis is that there is a phenomenon here that constitutes an existential threat.[61]

Crucially, Laor distinguished a racist rationale in Yaalon's logic: 'Do not mistake him: he is not saying that acts of terrorism pose a strategic threat to Israel. His is more of a prognosis than a diagnosis: the Palestinian *people* are a strategic threat. They are the cancer, and they must be removed.'[62] The notion of Palestinian society as a 'sick' society is becoming increasingly acceptable in political and academic circles; for example, Israeli deputy defence minister Zeev Boim was quoted saying that Palestinians probably commit terror attacks due to a 'genetic defect'.[63]

Of course, the possibility of personal mobility is crucial in a context of hardening racial conditions, where the notion of 'Palestinian terror' is deployed as a racializing category and as a strategy of social control within both the colonial Occupied Territories and Israel proper. It is then on the issue of Palestinian (lack of) mobility that the dynamics of apartheid are most strikingly reproduced. In his analysis of the pattern of control that Israel has established over the eastern part of Jerusalem, the West Bank and Gaza, Israeli anthropologist and geographer Halper has highlighted the role of the permanent road network established over Palestinian areas:

> As mechanisms of control, roads are ideal. They are permanent structures. They flow through long stretches of territory, inducing a feeling of natural connectedness, yet they effectively claim and monopolize land by their very routes. Roads are banal. They can be made to look inoffensive and even benign and attractive – or, if need be, they can be made to look like imposing and intimidating barriers. They can be opened or closed, and used as a means to separate, unite or channel populations, instruments of control or development.[64]

In the end, it is the road network linking the different settlements with each other and with Israel that more than anything else epitomizes segregation, as they are routes that cannot be used by anyone lacking a specific ethnic characterization.[65] As Derek Gregory has perceptively noted, these roads exemplify in the West Bank 'the proliferating partitions of colonial modernity':

> Palestinians know this every time they try to make an ordinary journey that once took them an hour and now takes a day (or more), if it can be made at all; there are no longer any ordinary journeys in the occupied territories. As the modern by-pass roads compress time and space for Israel's illegal settlers, so the dislocated minor roads and dirt tracks, the chokepoints and checkpoints, expand time and space for the Palestinians.[66]

It should be emphasized that a system of horizontal mobility that is based on a racial rationale is the very base of any segregationist regime.[67] Of course, the racialized system of mobility represented by settler-only roads should be associated with a corresponding and generalized pattern of mobility limitations continuously in place for Palestinians: curfews, closures, roadblocks, etc.[68] In the end, the permanent grid of bypass roads and settlements, associated with an institutionalized system of permits, checkpoints and closures, has progressively imposed on Palestinian mobility conditions similar to those of black South Africans dealing with the Pass Laws.

These trends, which already existed in the Oslo years, were further reinforced by Israeli responses to the Second Intifada.[69] As a result and for the first time, every movement by a Palestinian civilian within and outside the Occupied Territories was made conditional upon a specific permit. Checkpoints have been especially instrumental to this process. In another article, Laor subverted established narratives and pointed out that the

> ... checkpoints are not a product of the intifada. They were born in 1991, two years before the Oslo Accords, and were greatly reinforced after these agreements were signed ... The checkpoint system is not part of the intifada, but it did grow and strengthen 'thanks' to it. The checkpoint system is also not going to end when the intifada is over. The checkpoint system belongs entirely to the Israeli unwillingness to give up all of the territory of the West Bank, including all of the settlements. The checkpoint system is aimed at ensuring Israeli control over the lives of the Palestinians. Thus, it was strengthened after the signing of the Oslo Accords.
>
> From this perspective, the settlements are not the reason for the checkpoints. The 'isolated' settlements and the settlement blocs – part of the 'new' consensus of the Oslo era – are the pretext for the checkpoints, but they reveal their real function: We are present everywhere, we will split the Palestinian territory in every way, we will control them.[70]

Since the 1990s, Palestinians witnessed the multiplication of the administrative regimes for all Palestinian subjects. The years of the Second Intifada intensified this trend, adding to the equation the 'separation' barrier and the necessities brought about by an occupying army fully committed to making life for all Palestinians as unbearable as possible. More than in the past, they have become colonially subjected to a plethora of different legal conditions. In Israel proper, the multiplication of officially endorsed Arab subjectivities and administrative regimes (especially in relation to the requirement of serving in the army) is typical of a colonial regime: there are official divisions between Muslim, Druze and Christian Israeli Arabs, and further divisions between Bedouins and Muslim Israeli Arabs. On the other hand, one has to add the multiplication of statuses established for Palestinians in the Occupied Territories: those residing in the West Bank and residents of the Gaza Strip, refugees and non-refugees, permit holders and those who do not hold a permit, residents of areas A, B or C, and residents of East Jerusalem. Then there is the further bureaucratic differentiation introduced by the 'separation' fence.[71] There are those who can transit in areas under undivided Israeli military control, the few who can transit through Israel, those who can cross the 'separation' fence and get to their fields, those that must not even hope to re-enter any part of Palestine, and those who cannot move from home. To this maze, one should also add all the different and shifting combinations determined by the intersection of Israeli and Palestinian Authority, military and civilian, local and national controls: racially selective lines become stricter while a colonial regime and its associated segregation are progressively reinforced. Occupied Territories correspondent Amira Hass's description of the Qalandiyah checkpoint exemplifies a distressing reality:

> Residents of Jerusalem who hold blue identity cards are permitted to cross. Also permitted are residents of the West Bank who live in villages in the Ramallah area and hold orange identity cards. It is

forbidden for men 35 or older whose orange identity cards indicate
that they are residents of Hebron, Abu Dis, Jenin, Nablus or
Bethlehem. Several dozen such men tried their luck and sought to
cross, appealing to the hearts of the soldiers. Someone fabricated
a story about always being permitted to cross here, another said
'rain' and a third declared angrily: 'You are the occupiers in our
country and don't let me pass.' A fourth person tried to say that
he didn't have the money to pay for a taxi that would make the
50-kilometer detour to bring him to his home.

'We are acting according to the law,' the soldiers standing at the
breach responded. One spoke in a native Israeli accent, another
in Russian-accented Hebrew. 'What law are you talking about?' a
young man from Nablus asked in anger, in excellent Hebrew.[72]

Her conclusion, that 'The young soldiers at Qalandiyah who
permit or forbid passage with the wave of a hand are tools
serving a policy of annexation and dissection, wrapped in the
guise of security', seems reasonable. Of course, annexation and
dissection – literally, apartheid – in this case go together.

Bishop Desmond Tutu expressed his feelings after a visit
to Israel: 'It reminded me so much of what happened to us
black people in South Africa. I have seen the humiliation of
the Palestinians at checkpoints and roadblocks, suffering
like us when young white police officers prevented us from
moving about.'[73] In a few sentences, the South African Nobel
Laureate managed to pinpoint the two characteristic elements
of apartheid: a racialized constituency of humiliation and
restriction of movement.

3

The Troubles of Decolonization: France/Algeria, Israel/Palestine

Here is one major contradiction of a complicated circumstance: while a separation of the colonial space may now be unfeasible, as in the case of colonial South Africa, at the same time, a partition of Israel/Palestine still seems unavoidable. A comparative analysis involving a bi-national body politic now engaged in a process of national reconciliation and characterized by a degree of power-sharing between distinct communities should then be paralleled with an analysis of a context in which a resolution of the colonial dispute resulted in the establishment of a successor polity and in a process entailing an 'unmixing of peoples'.[1] After South Africa, the end of French Algeria can provide another significant departure.

This comparison is not unprecedented. For example, Herb Keinon of the *Jerusalem Post* reported that

> ... [when he was foreign minister] Binyamin Netanyahu noted that the Europeans [often] equated Israel's presence in the territories to France's colonialization of Algeria, forgetting that Israel's ties to Judea and Samaria go a bit deeper than France's 100-year connection to Algeria; that the Algerians never claimed Paris as their capital; and they certainly were never committed to wiping France off the map.[2]

Symptomatically, however, this perspective dangerously collapses Israel and Jewry in a way very similar to the way in

41

which 'French Algeria' was subsumed with 'France', and, of course, post-1967 settlements in the Occupied Territories have a much shorter history than French colonialism in Algeria. At the same time, while Algerian nationalism was not expecting to establish itself in Paris, it was certainly envisaging Algiers – the capital city of French Algeria – as the capital city of independent Algeria (and indeed, one could argue that East Jerusalem *is* the capital of the Israeli occupation).[3]

Indeed, since his first election as Prime Minister of Israel, and especially after the first publication of the Gaza 'disengagement' plan in February 2004, many have paid lip service to the possibility that Sharon may become an Israeli Charles de Gaulle. Sharon 'has not', 'must not, 'should not', 'cannot', 'wants to', become an Israeli de Gaulle.[4] This has become a powerful and resilient image, a trope that survived escalations in the conflict, targeted assassinations of Palestinian leaders and prolonged military activities in Gaza and in the West Bank.[5]

Like de Gaulle, Sharon is a prime minister with a very significant military history – a 'security man' and possibly a national icon enjoying (even more so after his second election) at least on paper an almost unprecedented parliamentary majority and a dependable number of political options. However, while at least at the level of reference, the de Gaulle/Sharon refrain has become a recurrent one, the comparative analysis of current Israeli and 1950s/early 1960s French/Algerian circumstances have been rare.[6]

This chapter proposes a comparative analysis of two conflicts in which a settler project supported by a colonial power reluctant to relinquish control over an area it deems strategically and ideologically essential for its survival was/is opposed to a loosely centralized nationalist movement struggling for independence.[7] In this context, a reading of French engagements in Algeria and the ways in which it shaped the institutional transition to the Fifth Republic may shed light on current contestations in Israel and in the Occupied Territories.[8] The first section of this chapter proposes a number of departures for a comparative analysis; the second section outlines the development and deployment in an Algerian context of French anti-insurgency military doctrines and draws a parallel with Israeli repressive stances *vis-à-vis* Palestinian insurgency and demands. The third part addresses the issue of narrative in the current conditions of the Israeli–Palestinian struggle.

Comparing Wars of Decolonization

A comparative approach should be aware of the obvious differences between Algeria in the 1950s and the current situation of Israel/Palestine. It should first consider a structurally dissimilar pattern of international relations, characterized now by unchallenged US hegemony and by an emerging neo-imperial strand in policies, sensibilities, postures and debates, as opposed to the much more developed anti-colonial rhetoric that was typical of US foreign engagements during the 1950s. Moreover, the guarantees the US has made available to Israel in its anti-insurgency campaign should be contrasted with the eventual discontinuation of support for France's colonial struggle in Algeria and elsewhere. Unlike de Gaulle's, Sharon's leadership took advantage from the unparalleled support of the US administration, including a groundbreaking endorsement for settlement annexation in the West Bank. Besides Cold War politics, the role played by the US emerges as an essential factor for an understanding of the differences between the two contexts.[9]

Beyond the constraints of the international context, one should also consider the obvious difference represented by the existence in 1950s France of a strong, vocal, organized and lucid opposition to colonialism, in contrast to the apathy that characterizes Israel's peace movement and political left.

As well, one should refer to Algeria's relatively peripheral location with respect to metropolitan France as opposed to the strategic position and the ideological/religious/national value the West Bank represents for Israel. The internal dynamics of the Palestinian and Algerian resistance organizations are also significantly different, with the Front de Libération Nationale (FLN) capable of enforcing a much higher degree of internal cohesion than the Palestine Liberation Organization (PLO).

Finally, in appraising the difference between the two scenarios, the nature of social/political processes should also be considered. During the 1950s, France was undergoing a rapid process of modernization, and, as argued for example by Kristin Ross in her sophisticated analysis of post-war French politics and cultural production, decolonization constituted an essential passage in this process.[10] While she conceptualized loss of empire as possibly the most relevant feature in determining emerging cultural and social patterns, it is unlikely that Israeli society is now undergoing a similar type of transition (unless one is willing to consider the demise of a once-comprehensive welfare state and growing fundamentalist tendencies as one such transformation).

In more general terms, however, it is possible to detect a number of historical parallelisms in the developing of the two colonial circumstances. For example, important discursive markers which are a shared feature of the two contexts relate to claims that an Algerian and a Palestinian nationality did not pre-exist the successful establishment of a colonial project, and to parallel imaginings of population transfer and of a final separation of peoples and/or of the colonial space (despite an intense elaboration, a proposed partition of the Algerian polity could not be pursued and was eventually abandoned).[11] Moreover, the articulation between recent migrants, Orthodox, European Jews and communities of Middle Eastern origin and their different relation with the settlement project can be associated with a division between Southern France – and the rest of a Mediterranean diaspora including Italians, Maltese, Corsicans, Spanish, Portuguese and Jews – and Northern France, relatively much less interested in retaining French Algeria at all costs.

The international political climate in which these conflicts developed also presents a number of similarities, including the intersections between the war of decolonization in Algeria and the Cold War on the one hand, and the Second Intifada and the post-9/11 global/permanent war on terror on the other. At the international level, one can also detect a similarity in the connection between France's loss of colonial sovereignty over Tunisia and Morocco and the successive emergence of an Algerian struggle for independence, and the Israeli withdrawal from southern Lebanon and the current Palestinian uprising. The disengagement of French forces in Vietnam was followed six months later by the military uprising of the FLN in Algeria. As many critics of the Israeli departure from Southern Lebanon have pointed out, there may be a relation between that Israeli redeployment and the military slant of the Second Intifada. (On the other hand, it has now emerged that, during the first few days of the uprising, Israeli soldiers in the Occupied Territories used no less than 1,300,000 bullets; this 'astounding statistic' could also contribute towards explaining the militarized character of the Palestinian resistance.)[12]

A comparative analysis is also justified in the light of Sharon's blend of might and withdrawal, a posture that resonates with the development of an autonomous strategic capability as it was instituted by France during de Gaulle's second presidency. Even the details of some of the events bear a remarkable resemblance, as in the case of the *Karin A*, seized in early 2002 by the Israeli navy while on route to Gaza with a cargo of weapons purportedly for the use of the Palestinian Authority, which corresponds to the ship sent by Egyptian President Abdel Nasser to help the Algerian resistance (that ship was also seized on approaching the zone of operations), or in the case of the Morice Line, built by the French at the border with Tunisia, with its electrified wire entanglements, floodlights, radar detection and minefields, which in many ways resemble the fence/wall currently being built in the West Bank.[13]

Two episodes involving non-Jewish IDF personnel in late 2004 further underscored the reality of a typically colonial war. After a successful attack that killed five Israeli soldiers belonging to the Desert Reconnaissance Battalion in southern Gaza, the practice of placing all Arab recruits volunteering for military service in ethnically separate units emerged as well as the fact that these units are permanently stationed in combat zones instead of being normally replaced like all other units.[14] The case of the Druze commander of a military outpost also in the Gaza Strip who 'confirmed' the killing of a 13-year-old girl (that is, she was shot repeatedly after she had already been hit and was lying on the ground) and was denounced by his Jewish subordinates was reported in Israeli media with racially informed overtones regarding the perceived inhumanity of soldiers incapable of respecting the 'values' of the Jewish army.[15] Both instances allow a comparative approach with the military performance of *harkis* units in Algeria (that is, non-French military personnel) and the concerns they raised in France.[16]

Debates over the nature of political leadership also present similarities between the two contexts. The new Israeli electoral system of direct election of the prime minister, partially dispensing with the traditional interference of party apparatuses, and the use of referendums, such as the one carried out among Likud Party members over the Gaza disengagement plan, or their recurrent prospect, are developments that resemble the many referendums that were used in France under de Gaulle and the direct – almost personal – typology of political forms that characterized the transition between the Fourth and the Fifth Republics. In 'The Frogs who Demand a King' Sartre brilliantly analyses 'Gaullism' and the ways in which the democratic institutions of republican France were distorted during the years of the Algerian war.[17] In this respect, there are also similarities in relation to public attitudes toward Sharon and his leadership and the expectations that his conversion to peace rhetoric did raise in sections of the political left in Israel and abroad.

Another point of departure for a comparative analysis is that in both scenarios significant public and intellectual debates became eventually concerned at the ways in which these conflicts were eroding important democratic freedoms in their respective metropolitan systems. There is a noticeable resonance between Sartre's commentaries, which emphasize both the impasse in which France's political and economic structures were caught and the fact that French democratic life was being critically undermined by the war effort – the unfinished business of decolonization, and references to the fact that occupation and repression are sapping the very fabric of Israeli moral and democratic life – the unfinished business of post-Zionism.[18] In this respect, Sartre's bitter criticism of the traditional left for its ambiguities in facing colonial issues may facilitate the interpretation of current political stalemates and debates in Israel.[19] As well, one could draw a parallel between the breaking of established patterns of public behaviour regarding military and patriotic duties represented by the 'Manifesto of the 121' of 1960 – when prominent figures explicitly invited conscripts to desert the army – and the public letter signed by 27 Israeli Air Force pilots published in October 2003.[20]

Public disagreements between the prime minister's office and the leadership of the IDF over the admissibility and details of the evacuation of settlers and military installations from Gaza and areas of the West Bank, and over the procedure with which the disengagement plan was decided upon, should also be mentioned.[21] Divisions between the prime minister and the IDF chief of staff have indeed reproduced a political dynamic similar to the growing contradiction between army milieus and de Gaulle's presidency when it became clear, after a long and troubled deliberation, that he was prepared to allow for the full independence of an Algerian polity.[22] The apparent collusion of relevant sectors of the IDF with the settler movement, and obvious signs of insubordination approaching the Gaza pullout of the summer of 2005, also fit well in this comparative outline.[23]

The traditional availability, currency and mobilization of army rhetoric, representing a higher, purer morality – the morality of a sounder *pays réel*, an image above the criticism emanating from a sick society with a corrupt legality – is indeed another very important shared feature of the two contexts.[24] Again, Sartre perceptively notes how the role of the French army in Algeria was essential to its very existence, that the army 'will never leave Algeria, its ultimate justification, its interest as a corps', and how (previous to the decision of abandoning Algeria) 'the [French] executive is in fact in Algiers; it is composed of civilians and soldiers, and decides about France on the basis of Algeria'.[25] Recurrent denunciations of a settler capacity for determining political processes and national priorities against the inclinations of a majority of Israeli citizens could indeed support the argument that the Israeli executive also resides in the settlements, is composed of civilians and soldiers, and decides about Israel on the basis of the settlement enterprise.

The growing prospect of civil confrontation and settler violence – in fact, its perceived inevitability, as the prospected pullout from Gaza neared – provides yet another element that would invite a comparative approach. While a tense debate surrounding the possibility of violent resistance against any evacuation immediately followed Sharon's announcement, these hypothetical scenarios, raising fears of civil war and a split in the army, are reminiscent of the emergence and functioning of the Organisation Armée Secrète (OAS), a typically settler terrorist organization, and of the failed *coup* in Algiers of April 1961. Importantly, the declared attempt of the generals' *coup* in Algiers was aimed at creating a 'French form of Israel after a three-month pacification of the rural areas'. The generals expected that eventually 'France and the world would recognize this state and restore it to the fold.'[26] And it seems fair to say that Israeli settler organizations are also aiming at creating the very powerful spectre of an Israeli form of French Algeria.[27] Some in the settlers' camp may be even considering a 'Rhodesian' option.[28] These are threatening scenarios that, according to settlers and their political supporters, Israel and the world would eventually come to recognize and avoid by restoring the settler enterprise to the fold and to the general consensus.[29] Describing an 'unprecedented trauma of identity' (that is, anti-pullout rallies), normally sober commentators have used apocalyptictones:

> They stood in long lines, the youths of the rule of law and the youths of total belief. One was silent and scared, the other was pressuring for refusal. One was idle, the other was calling out, 'Jews don't banish Jews'.
>
> At 9:30 P.M., Border Police officers stopped the orange march, two kilometers from Netivot. Was there really a need? Was it right to use Israel Defense Forces soldiers to stop a civilian rally inside sovereign Israeli territory?
>
> At 10:30 P.M., none of this mattered. The dynamics of arbitrariness on the one hand and unsupervised rebellion on the other had taken their toll. Spread out on the yellow fields was a sight that looked like it came out of pictures of wars in the Middle Ages. There were long lines of police officers and soldiers and

Border Police officers, and there were masses of religious warriors. And the cry echoing into the night: 'Soldier, police officer – refuse orders. Soldier, police officer – refuse orders.'

Will Israel survive this summer? ...[30]

While it should be noted that a theatrical dimension was never absent from the politics of Israeli settlers, the split between supporters of the disengagement and its opponents may be less marked than it would appear. Besides a self-proclaimed and pre-emptively declared national trauma, the evacuation of the Gaza settlements in August 2005 could also be construed as a collective Apotropaic ritual in which everyone plays a specific part: the evacuators, the evacuees, their respective supporters, their different colours and ribbons, the media frenzy preceding and surrounding the event, a generalized and intimate and yet highly externalized turmoil, the suspense of not knowing whether the evacuation would actually happen or be postponed, all converge into a collective exorcism in which a settler society incessantly experiences the end of the occupation in order to avoid actually facing its demise.

Winning the Wars of Decolonization

Most of all, however, a parallel situation between the two scenarios is to be detected in the respective position of an army that could not win decisively the numerous wars it was engaged during preceding decades – with no fault of its own, according to a widespread perception in military circles – while losing almost no battle.[31] One Israeli army commander in Gaza was reported to state: 'We are winning in this conflict. In the military arena we are winning every day, several times.'[32] However perplexing, this statement is in many ways typical of military personnel engaged in a low-intensity anti-colonial war that can not be decisively concluded. Similar states of mind were often expressed in different colonial contexts by military officers trying to come to terms with a reality they failed to recognize fully.

Chief of Staff Moshe Yaalon's interview to *Haaretz*, released on the eve of his departure from office, confirms another interpretative impasse. Before the outbreak of the Second Intifada, he had become aware that war was inevitable:

> ... [during the Oslo period] I reached the conclusion that we were in a situation of reverse asymmetry. That we were in retreat, whereas the Palestinians were on the offensive. Therefore I thought that our mission was to create a wall in the face of the Palestinians. To prove to them that terrorism does not pay. Yes, to burn that into their consciousness – even if there are some who do not like that term.[33]

He was now drawing a balance of intense years of anti-insurgency achievements. Yet, despite a glowing assessment of an increased repressive capacity ('the freedom of action we acquired as a result of taking control of the territory was what generated the turnabout. It reduced the number of casualties; reinforced our staying power; improved the economic situation; and obtained international legitimization'), he concluded by noting that 'despite their military weakness, the Palestinians feel that they are making progress'.[34]

It must be daunting: despite an anti-insurgency that had been carefully prepared, and regardless of years of unrelenting success, his assessment remained the same he had before the Intifada: 'reversed asymmetry' (that is, being the strongest and losing ground).

> Despite their military weakness, the Palestinians feel they are making progress. Whereas we are waging a battle of withdrawal and delay ... We are retreating without our having a narrative. Without our having an agreed story. Look, the whole question is whether your withdrawal is perceived by the other side as an act of choice or an act of flight. If it is perceived as a flight, they will continue to come after you; if it is perceived as a choice, everything looks different. As of today, three months before the disengagement, it is still not clear whether they will treat it as a flight or as a choice.[35]

A growing awareness that the Palestinian uprising could not be ultimately and militarily terminated sets indeed a comparative tone with French Algeria. Attempts to 'sear into' the Palestinian consciousness the uselessness of resistance against the occupation especially invite a comparison between two military strategies.[36] The indecisive nature of many of the operations recently carried out in Gaza also supports this approach; an operation aimed at 'provoking armed men into exposing themselves', such as the IDF's Gaza operation carried out during March 2004 (though one could mention many more instances), may be indicative of an attempt to restore a type of deterrence that is perceived as somewhat in decline.[37]

The exchange in the summer of 2004 between the head of Military Intelligence and Shin Bet security service chief regarding whether the 'terror barrel' has a bottom or not, whether it is possible to envisage a permanent eradication of the 'terror infrastructure', or whether anti-insurgency could only provide an enhanced capacity for containment, also epitomizes a strategic impasse.[38]

One *Haaretz* editorial has synthesized this understanding and called for a reversal of policy:

> The lesson from dozens of similar operations, which intensified the desire for revenge, produced many suicide bombers and led to attacks that killed hundreds of Israelis. Dozens of assassinations, hundreds of house demolitions, and tens of thousands unemployed did not do a thing to improve Israel's deterrent force in the territories. The time has come for the makers of policy and those who implement it to drop the illusion of a military solution to the conflict; until a political solution is found, they should take care to make wise and controlled use of force.[39]

This would indeed be major departure from an established and long-lasting tradition. Throughout the 1990s, the option of a repressive war against the Palestinians was left open. After an ongoing preparation that was never abandoned in the years of the Oslo process (in case of a breakdown in negotiations, but this eventually became a self-fulfilling prophecy), an updated anti-insurgency doctrine was finally and systematically tested during the first four years of the Second Palestinian Intifada.[40]

Quite significantly, the lessons of Algeria seem to have been taken on board: indeed, a number of aspects characterizing the strategic approach the IDF has developed do resemble the French military doctrine as it was practiced in Algeria during the 1950s.[41] This was a Manichean all-embracing military doctrine where 'good' fights 'evil', unsurprisingly, a precursor to more contemporary approaches to anti-terrorist rhetoric.[42] In the words of military historian Anthony Clayton:

> In total counter-revolutionary war, all means could be justified and order should precede law; military needs must override all legal and political factors, and in the last resort the military might have to dominate the political leadership ... Any counter-insurgency campaign had therefore to be fought with intelligence and psychological warfare agencies that could operate without restraint. At any local level communities could be deported or interned, individuals detained and subjected to severe interrogation, measures that in practice very quickly turned to semi-legalized brutality. Intelligence and military priority targets were to be insurgents' area command and logistic structures and key local insurgent personalities, either for assassination or capture for interrogation or for psychological re-education and use; the domination of areas to keep insurgents on the run; and remorseless local counter-terror in the case of ambushes or bomb attacks.[43]

It should be emphasized that the systematic performance of this type of warfare represents without a doubt a considerable achievement in both contexts.[44] While General Challe's reassertion strategy during 1959 produced one of the most effective counter-insurgency campaigns ever executed, this operational assessment is also valid with regards to the Israelis flexible reoccupation of Area A of the West Bank.

The strategic approach of the two anti-insurgency efforts also supports a comparative analysis. In a *New York Review of Books* piece, Robert Malley and Hussein Agha have noted an

important aspect of the ways the Second Palestinian Intifada has
been dealt with and a defining feature of all colonial wars:

> Ariel Sharon has won the current round of the Israeli–Palestinian
> conflict. His goal, an age-old objective, was for Palestinians to tire
> of their national struggle. To bring about the impoverishment and
> despair of the Palestinian people was never his purpose as such, but
> he viewed that result as a prerequisite to diverting the Palestinians'
> concentration from political issues to mundane matters of more
> immediate, quotidian concern.[45]

A French counter-insurgency effort had also systematically
and successfully tried to shift the attention of insurgents' and
the general population from a preoccupation with national
aspirations to a reality of deprivation and to link an end of
challenge with an improvement of living conditions.
Besides this well-tried approach, it is the very stages with
which the French Army could defeat the Algerian insurgency
– initial disarticulation of urban resistance, isolation of resisters
and of their political organizations from external support, and,
finally, systematic destruction of enemy capabilities through
'nomad' units capable of searching and destroying enemy targets
– that have been reproduced in the West Bank and Gaza. Initial
invasion of Palestinian population centres (Operation Defensive
Shield) was followed by progressive domestic and international
marginalization of Palestinian nationalist organizations ('There
is no partner'), by an intense activity aimed at the destruction
of smuggling tunnels in Gaza, and by continuous incursions in
Palestinian population centres.[46] A coherent policy of targeted
assassinations of political cadres and cell leaders is also an
apparent feature of both anti-insurgency practices. In the end,
in both conflicts, from a perceived initial insurgency advantage,
the military balances were progressively and surely shifted to
an increasing and eventually unrestrained capacity for 'pre-
emptive' containment.
By the end of 1958, the anti-colonial Armée de Libération
Nationale was approaching total military defeat. By mid-

1959 this defeat was almost total. What saved Algerian nationalism was its remaining politically and internationally irreplaceable; exactly the two factors that are ensuring that a Palestinian political option remain capable of challenging Israeli unilateralism. An emerging pattern of Israeli military success against the Intifada resonates with the nature of French military success: an accomplishment which, however, solves none of the political problems. Indeed, military success had ultimately made sections of the army and the settler movements in Algeria believe that now that they had won, they had to secure their achievements by controlling political processes.

In any case – and this should also be emphasized – in both contexts, an astounding repressive capacity could not ultimately upset the political balance. Clayton, for example, observed that 'In claiming that they were winning the fighting on the ground the elite force commanders were already confusing local military success and an overall military re-assertion over most of Algeria with suppression of the rebellion, a confusion to worsen in the next year.'[47]

While this could be one feature of the current situation in the West Bank and Gaza, an analytical capacity for distinguishing between military achievements and ensuring the availability of political options becomes essential in a comparison between the two circumstances. Already in November 2003 a number of former heads of the Shin Bet warned the government of the risks of fighting terrorism in a political vacuum and without the prospect of a political solution.[48]

Indeed, whether Israel has won its anti-insurgency campaign in the West Bank and Gaza has been recurrently debated.[49] On the one hand, a prominent piece by Charles Krauthammer appeared in the *Washington Post* and announced Israel's victory: 'While no one was looking, something historic happened in the Middle East. The Palestinian intifada is over, and Palestinians have lost ... The intent of the intifada was to demoralize Israel, destroy its economy, bring it to its knees, and thus force it to withdraw and surrender to Palestinian demands, just as Israel withdrew in defeat from Southern Lebanon in May 2000.'[50]

Krauthammer's conclusion was based on a quantitative analysis of the number of Israeli casualties Palestinian attacks could exact. And yet, his argument over the aims of Palestinian resistance could be reversed: the repressive campaign that was initiated *before* the consolidation of the Intifada was also aimed at demoralizing the Palestinian camp and at destroying the Palestinian economy and thus force its leadership to surrender to Israeli demands, *unlike* Southern Lebanon. (One could argue, in fact, that the 'spectre' of Southern Lebanon seems to be a currently more active trope in an Israeli consciousness than in a Palestinian one, and that as a refrain it is activated in a manner very similar to the ways in which the precedent of Indochina was mobilized in support of the French effort during the war in Algeria.) In the end and despite Krauthammer's logic, while the Palestinians have certainly lost, Israel did not win.[51]

On the other hand, *Haaretz* analyst Aluf Benn has been able to pinpoint an Israeli incapacity of transforming military achievements into political success, an inability that affected French negotiating efforts as well:

> Israel has succeeded in restraining terror, but it has failed to translate its tactical success into a strategic victory. The Palestinians have not caved in, despite the devastating blows they have endured. Facing Israel's military superiority, the Palestinians have turned for support to the international arena ...
>
> Sharon invested tremendous effort in his personal fight against Arafat. The Palestinian leader is confined in his Ramallah compound, and the international community has somehow become accustomed to this situation. But what good does this really do? ... Arafat remains the Palestinian leader; his message has not changed, and nobody around him will be content with anything less than Israeli withdrawal from all the territories and some sort of right of refugee return.[52]

It should be noted that a dissonance between military achievements and political success is a long-lasting feature of colonial warfare. De Gaulle finally accepted the need for serious negotiation with the FLN only after it had become apparent that the search for an alternative leadership could not produce results. Israel could also degrade Palestinian political organizations but not replace them. Besides, as noted in a *Guardian* article by Kevin Toolis, author of *Rebel Hearts: Journeys Within the IRA's Soul*, 'you can't make a deal with the dead.'[53]

Narratives of the Wars of Decolonization

Ultimately, the strategic terrain also shifts, and the very possibility that sections of the Palestinian public may develop a 'victory narrative' in the face of a possible Israeli withdrawal – as happened in Lebanon – has now become an essential feature in determining the pattern and evolution of the conflict.

Haaretz journalist Amir Oren, who published a number of articles on the interest the Israeli military is showing in the determination of historical narratives through the targeted use of military operations, noted this shift and suggested that a pre-emptive attention to narrative-shaping is informing both the choices of the Palestinian resistance and those of the Israeli repression. He pointed to the strong connection between the possible withdrawal and the wave of violence that engulfed the Gaza Strip since its announcement and noted that the 'Palestinian organizations wish to shape in their own spirit the story of the IDF's withdrawal.'[54] But this is of course also true of the Israeli military: they also need to shape a suitable narrative of their possible redeployment.[55] While the fight could potentially escalate once more, already, at least in part, it has moved to the sphere of historical interpretation – a development that does not see Israeli military authorities unprepared.[56]

More generally, the power of narrative in the context of colonialism was compellingly addressed by Said in *Culture and Imperialism*:

> A great deal of recent criticism has concentrated on narrative fiction, yet very little attention has been paid to its position in the history and world of empire ...|The main battle in imperialism is over land, of course; but when it came to who owned the land, who had the right to settle and work on it, who kept it going, who won it back, and who now plans its future – these issues were reflected, contested, and even for a time decided in narrative.[57]

On the other hand, Said also noted that the outright absence of a common narrative constitutes one of the most demoralizing aspects of the relationship between Palestinian and Israeli discourses. With regards to establishing a shared narrative, Said had even proposed a meeting of intellectuals in order to establish a minimum common-denominator historical version:

> Might it not make sense for a group of respected historians and intellectuals, composed equally of Palestinians and Israelis, to hold a series of meetings to try to agree to a modicum of truth about this conflict, to see whether the known sources can guide the two sides to agree on a body of facts – who took what from whom, who did what to whom, and so on – which in turn might reveal a way out of the present impasse?[58]

However, a common if highly contested narrative of sorts may yet be emerging as one of the outcomes of the daily killings in Israel/Palestine. It is a narrative in which any Israeli withdrawal, or its prospect, is brought about by a shift in the dynamics of insurgency and repression.

Quite crucially, narrative is also a matter of perception.[59] Besides a dire reality of bitter defeat, the establishment of a Palestinian victory narrative (a development that could allow territorial compromise as it allowed Egyptian President Anwar Sadat to engage in a peace process with Israel after the 1973 War) was welcomed by Danny Rubinstein in a *Haaretz* piece in January 2005:

Between the sense of victory in Egypt at that time and the way the Palestinians perceive the disengagement plan, there is an abyss – but there is one point that is the same: the disengagement is perceived in Gaza and the West Bank as a great victory. The Israeli explanations that it is a 'disengagement' and not a withdrawal, and certainly not a retreat, do not interest the Palestinians. As far as they are concerned, the army is going to quit the entire Gaza Strip and the State of Israel will be uprooting the settlements. Throughout all the years of the peace process, that has never happened. All the complicated negotiations, all the summits and all the diplomatic talks never achieved for the Palestinians what the armed struggle and resistance achieved: a disengagement.[60]

At the same time, it is a narrative of unilateral acts and relentless reciprocity. It is a narrative whose dynamics replicate those characterizing the war in Algeria, a common narrative made up of the exemplary repetition of helicopter missile strikes and of suicide attacks. (This includes their more intangible surrogates/more refined substitutes: the unmanned drones guided by military personnel located tens of kilometres away – capable of releasing non-propelled missiles that reveal their presence only when they explode – and the Qassam rockets, one replacement for suicide bombing in an age of increasingly impenetrable barriers, and an indicator of a necessity of preserving an appearance of symmetry in the suffering of the Palestinian and Israeli communities.)

As suggested in the introduction, Fanon dealt with settler and anti-colonial violence and narrative in a way that is perhaps suitable for the interpretation of the Israeli/Palestinian conflict (in *Culture and Imperialism*, Said quotes extensively from *The Wretched of the Earth*, but this book was written before the Oslo years, and Said could not predict its relevance in the case of the Israeli/Palestinian situation in the years of the Second Intifada):

The settler makes history and is conscious of making it. And because he constantly refers to the history of his mother country, he clearly indicates that he himself is the extension of the mother country. Thus the history which he writes is not the history of the country which he plunders but the history of his own nation in regard to all that she skins off, all that she violates and starves.

The immobility [later he speaks of apartheid as one of the forms of 'division into compartments': 'The native,' he adds, 'is being hemmed in ... The first thing which a native learns is to stay in his place'] to which the native is condemned can only be called in question if the native decides to put an end to the history of colonization – the history of pillage – and to bring into existence the history of the nation – the history of decolonization.[61]

Said recognizes that Fanon's intuition regarding violence, '"a cleansing force", which pits colonizer against colonized directly', involves the production and reproduction of narrative and that 'change can come about only when the native (like Lukacs's alienated worker) decides that colonization must end – in other words, there must be an epistemological revolution'.[62] In this process of synthesis, a narrative of decolonization may be established:

The violence of the colonial regime and the counter-violence of the native balance each other and respond to each other in an extraordinary reciprocal homogeneity ... The settler's work is to make even dreams of liberty impossible for the native. The native's work is to imagine all possible methods for destroying the settler. On the logical plane, the Manicheanism of the settler produces a Manicheanism of the natives, to the theory of the 'absolute evil of the native' the theory of the 'absolute evil of the settler' replies.[63]

These processes shaped the Algerian war of decolonization and have influenced Israel/Palestine during the Second Intifada. In the end, the French establishment could convincingly declare it had won the war against 'terror' in Algeria. Quite significantly, the negotiations of Evian were concluded with a number of measures that would protect French interests in independent Algeria. *Colons* would be granted double citizenship and full civic rights, special political representation, special courts, and no expropriation without indemnity would be allowed. In the end, however, all these negotiating achievements meant very little for the majority of *colons*; those who could, prepared their exodus, each family carrying out a tragic, painful, personal form of unilateral disengagement. The final deal between the negotiating teams allowed for a French garrison to be stationed in Algeria, and included a provision to share Saharan oil and to allow nuclear tests in the Sahara Desert. Despite this, news of the agreement was followed by OAS terrorist carnage and by the exodus of some 1,450,000 people to France. Settlers abandoned their property and had bonfires in the streets.

Ultimately, the military victory in the Battle of Algiers became associated with political defeat when it came to permanently dismantle the prospect of an independent Algeria. This is a predicament that may concern Israeli efforts as well: the IDF was indisputably able to win the 'Battle of Jenin' and to achieve a substantial reduction of the level of resistance in the Occupied Territories; however, this military capacity could not be translated into the possibility of enforcing a lasting settlement. (It should be noted that a striking parallelism is also mirrored in the political uses of Italian director Gillo Pontecorvo's famous movie *La Battaglia di Algieri* and Mohammed Bakri's 'controversial' film entitled *Jenin Jenin*.[64])

By starving itself of options and interlocutors, Israel may have reproduced French actions *vis-à-vis* Algerian nationalism. The typology of concerted decolonization that was envisaged by the Oslo process was eventually replaced by anti-colonial/ anti-insurgency practices with their characteristic accounting of death. A fledgling institutional imagination of decolonization was then radically reshaped.

In another context, Smuts Professor of the History of the British Commonwealth Donald Anthony Low's review of the contraction of the British Empire elaborates a largely positive if somewhat ambiguous narrative of decolonization, a characteristic he strictly associates with a British flexible practice of successful institutional transfer and capacity for

organizing constitutional arrangements for the devolution
of colonial authority and sovereignties.[65] During the 1990s,
and despite inevitable contradictions, a British-style variety
of decolonization (and associated neo-colonialist forms) had
appeared to be the issue with regards to Israel/Palestine. The
realities of a 'wretched of the earth' type of anti-colonial war
followed the failure of the Camp David negotiations in July
2000. As a result, a French-style tradition of decolonization
with a typical propensity for unilateralism was placed on
the agenda.[66]

Moreover, as noted in Chapter 1, in Israel, but also in the
Occupied Territories, since the 1990s there was a generalized
shift from assimilation to association in the administrative
regimes of Palestinian subjects. This colonial dichotomy was
originally explored by Raymond Betts in a 1961 book on
French colonial theory, but more recent historical research has
emphasized that the relationship between these two categories
is a very complex one and that French colonial policy was a
combination of conflicting tendencies.[67] While Alice Conklin
detected in French colonial history a move from assimilation
to association following the First World War, a similar
argument, highlighting both the traditional combination of
the two practices and a more recent shift in emphasis, could
be sustained in relation to the development of Israeli colonial
policies following the First Intifada. One consequence of this
convergence is that French colonial history is indeed relevant
to the current conditions of Israel/Palestine. US Secretary of
State Dean Rusk had feared in 1962 an 'Algerianization' of
the Arab–Israeli dispute.[68] While this prophecy may have
acquired some currency, one should note that this evolution
could be swiftly reversed, as post-Arafat Israeli stands may be
indicating. Swinging from one policy to the other, or pursuing
both at the same time, is a prerogative that colonial powers
always retain and often exercise.[69]

A radical transition to a non-colonialist institutional form
after a bitter war of decolonization is encountered in both the

end of the Fourth French Republic and the fall of the Salazar regime in Portugal.[70] Both these polities had been incapable of transforming their political structures in a way that would recognize the reality of a war that could not be won; or better, of a struggle that could be successfully waged but only at the cost of doing so indefinitely and at the inevitable cost of paying the price of a debilitating war of attrition. Already in the early 1960s Maghreb expert Jacques Berque had lamented how contemporaries could not understand that one particularity of colonial wars is that winning is worse than losing.[71]

2004 witnessed the fiftieth anniversary of the battle of Dien Bien Phu, a major breaking-point in the history of colonialism and decolonization. Sharon's 2004 Gaza disengagement plan also marked an unprecedented and possibly crucial passage. While its implementation raised images resonating with those of the end of French Algeria, the possibility of a new start in dealing with the conflict has to contend with Sharon's somewhat declining popularity and with the political constraints of a prime minister who must face a stubborn and growing resistance in dealing with his own party and widespread scepticism in dealing with other sections of the political spectrum.[72] While the Gaza settlers represent only 3 per cent of the whole settler population, it took the Israeli parliament 14 months to decide finally in March 2005 that there would be no referendum over the Gaza withdrawal. Rather than a new de Gaulle capable and willing of cutting the Gordian knot represented by a conflict that could not be won, Sharon may still pass into history as an Israeli Pflimlin: the last of the prime ministers of the French Fourth Republic.

4

Founding Violence and Settler Societies: Rewriting History in Israel and Australia

The notion that Israel/Palestine is in a situation where the politics of history acquire a special significance enjoys by now wide currency. Dennis Ross, for example, who served in various positions as a leading US diplomat in charge of the 'peace process' and was involved in the preparation and management of the failed Camp David summit (and who wrote an 850-page book on the negotiations), started his reconstruction with an intelligent presentation of the three narratives that inform the conflict: the Israelis, the Arabs and the Palestinians (the Palestinians last).[1] Of course, detecting how different collective memories diverge and their incompatibility does not necessarily require an appraisal of the ways in which a specific set of settler colonial relationships have shaped them.[2]

This chapter is about the rewriting of history and current perceptions. Departing from the assumption that in a settler context the struggle over narrative becomes an especially contested domain, this chapter constitutes an exercise in comparative historiography and deals with two processes of historiographical redescription in two settler determined polities: Israel and Australia. Although the historical experiences these debates refer to and the social and political environments in which they have developed share only a number of common features, they also share a number of defining characteristics. Among these similarities is the apparent standstill in the 'reconciliation' and 'peace' processes – whose irreversibility had been solemnly proclaimed in both cases at the beginning of the 1990s and yet remain unfulfilled. Also characterizing both debates, is the obvious incapacity of coming to terms with a history epitomized by extreme violence and denial. In each polity, the deadlock in the reconciliation process has been brought about by – among several other factors – the hegemony exercised by a right-wing electoral majority that finds expression in a government that clings anxiously and nostalgically to an ideology strongly related to settler, colonial and colonising practices.

While governments in both Israel and Australia – and, albeit to a lesser extent, their left-wing opponents – are sincerely convinced that they are proposing 'generous offers' to their Palestinian and Aboriginal counterparts, the prospect of a final settlement (the possibility of a 'treaty' in one case, a final-status peace agreement in the other) are continually postponed. As a result, in both cases, a resolution to the conflict tends to fade into an indefinite future. The only progress in both these appeasement processes remains the possibility that the ruling government may – however carefully – word a statement conveying some sense of regret for past injustices.

More than in the previous two chapters, selecting these case studies contradicts established perceptions.[3] On the Israeli side, this would generally be a result of a strong ideological assumption stressing the impossibility of comparative approaches involving Zionist history.[4] The suggestion that the Israeli experience in relation to the Palestinian people (that is, as a 'nation within', if one considers the consistent minority of Palestinians endowed with Israeli citizenship, and a nation under colonial rule, if the population of the Occupied Territories is considered) could be contextualized in the background of other colonial enterprises of settlement clashes with Zionist versions of an intrinsically unique history. On the Australian side, the reference to 'founding violence' and the comparison with the overblown brutality that characterizes the historical evolution of Israel/Palestine would also appear contentious. The last remnants of the Australian mythology of the 'quiet frontier' discourage a comparison with a situation characterized by such uncompromising hostility. As well as attachment to notions of 'pacific settlement', the very acknowledgement of violence to such a pervasive degree would suggest political and legislative action to compensate the indigenous population. Whatever the case may be, an old Palestinian man told the *National Geographic* in the early 1990s: 'You know we Palestinians are civilized peoples, but we are treated like aborigines [*sic*]'; there may be some truth in this.[5] At the same time, it would be difficult to deny that Aboriginal communities are remarkably sophisticated and are often treated like Palestinians.

Despite objections, the similarities between two processes of historical reappraisal and the debates that surrounded them – the 'history wars' of Israel and Australia – recommend a comparative approach at the historiographical level.[6] In *Against Paranoid Nationalism*, Ghassan Hage noted the 'paranoiac colonial sensibility one finds in colonial-settler nations that are in constant fear of decolonisation' and explicitly referred to the convergence of anxious nationalisms and colonial paranoias in Israel and Australia.[7] Yet perhaps the most important shared trait emerging from the comparison of these historiographical revisionisms is that, despite the deadlock in the evolution of the reconciliation/peace processes, the academic communities of both, or at least important sections of these communities, have repeatedly promoted notions significantly distant from both the political agendas of their governments, and from public perceptions. In both historiographies, a new generation of historians has collectively proposed interpretations departing dramatically from the orthodoxies entertained by both the majority of the population and their political representatives.

Both countries have witnessed a marked public reluctance to receive some of the conclusions the 'new historians' were proposing, especially when an appraisal of the 'founding violence' was involved. Master narratives are rarely replaced without a fight. An Israeli 'original sin' was heatedly discussed, and so it was in the case of Australia, where the reference to the term 'genocide', as it was used by the Human Rights and Equal Opportunity Commission in the *Bringing Them Home* report, was met with scandalized and apologetic reactions.[8] Such parallels may be explained by the fact that in both cases, historical inquiry into the violence on the 'frontier' brings into question the very foundations of the state and entails a reappraisal of the founding myths that support most orthodox narratives.[9] In the end, the Australian polemic over the 'black armband' interpretation of history is reproduced in a surprisingly similar fashion by Israeli academics at odds with established interpretative patterns.[10] Yet, and this should be emphasized, it is not merely a question wrought by a generation of historians working on the foundations of the state and on the settler/indigenous relationship in two different contexts. As I will try to demonstrate, while the debates that surrounded these processes also resonate to a surprising degree, the very dynamics of the processes of historiographical redescription were reproduced in a similar way.

Whereas it is apparent that the peace process initiated at Oslo has collapsed, this article assumes that Australia's native title legislation and 'Aboriginal reconciliation' have also failed to address the ultimate nature of Aboriginal dispossession. Aboriginal communities have had little, if any, access to their lands and have been forced to allocate important resources to have their titles considered.[11] Even the more recent and more reductive approach to 'practical reconciliation' has not delivered visible results. These are well-known facts; none the less, it remains important to highlight them.

The first and second sections of this chapter outline the evolution of two historiographical evolutions; the third section comments comparatively on a number of similarities between the two processes and on conflicting uses of the past in a settler context. This chapter argues that the two contexts share an unwillingness/impossibility to face the founding violence of a settler community, and a manifest inability of renovated historical narratives to command public opinion. In the end, the colonial imagination of these bodies politic proved resilient to the transformations of renewed historiographies.

The 'New' Israeli History

Until two decades ago a systematic historiography on the origins of the State of Israel did not exist. The very organization of the Israeli cultural establishment prevented autonomous and alternative historical research. Historical contributions and interpretations were published in a much ideologized context and in a situation in which the Mapai, the Zionist social democratic party, in power continuously between 1948 and 1977, hegemonized intellectual debates thanks to a system of rigid control over historical research – a control exercised through a close network of publishing houses, research institutes, kibbutzes, unions and other organizations.

Dissenting contributions with some historical content were coming from left-wing Zionist and non-Zionist parties, but – apart from the even more pronounced ideological conceptions they displayed – the interpretative orthodoxy remained unchallenged. On the one hand, Palestinians were not acknowledged, their invisible presence rarely addressed; they were subsumed within the larger issue of Israel's relationship with the Arab world while losing their historical autonomy and legitimacy. On the other hand – and as a consequence of this non-recognition – the history of the violent dispossession and expulsion of the Palestinian population that followed the establishment of the State of Israel in 1948–49 was subsumed under the history of the military campaigns Israel conducted against the Arab armies. Palestinian existence was practically denied, the history of Palestine prior to Zionist settlement and the Israeli–Arab conflict overlooked, accounts of Palestinian dispossession systematically disregarded: a far cry from the tense debate of the 1990s.[12]

The first important moment of challenge to this master narrative was perhaps the publication of Yehoshua Porath's *The Emergence of the Palestinian-Arab National Movement* in 1974.[13] The book explored the early phase of the Palestinian nationalist movement and argued for a comprehensive shift in the interpretation of its origins. By emphasizing the existence of such a movement in a period (the 1920s) in which a Palestinian political agency was typically denied, Porath was according Palestinian nationalism a history independent from both the Arab world and the Jewish presence. Significantly, in this work, Palestinians were accorded an autonomous political and historical development. And yet, this precursor work was published in a context of rigid orthodoxy: despite its groundbreaking character, the Israeli historical debate during the 1970s remained substantially constrained within the limits of an unyielding interpretation.

Paradoxically, the event that freed historical inquiry from the intellectual control exercised by the Zionist left was Menachem Begin's electoral victory in 1977.[14] While the right never developed the network that had assured the hegemony of left-wing Zionism in previous decades, a number of intellectuals started proposing interpretations and themes that would have been unthinkable in the cultural climate of previous decades.[15] Since then, a comprehensive process of historiographical redescription of the national record proceeded mainly along three thematic lines.[16]

One considered the problem of Palestinian refugees, whose fight for survival and acknowledgement involved a fight for the recognition of their historical experience.[17] Benny Morris's works, for example, have been essential in placing this problem on the intellectual and public agendas since the 1980s.[18] While until then Palestinian refugees had been erased from the historical record, this new interpretative trend managed to recover to an extent their experience and to propose it to the Israeli public.[19] Morris, using archival material, documented the deportation of Palestinian people during and in the aftermath of the 1948 conflict. In a following work, Morris has also raised the question of Palestinian 'infiltration' and showed how most of these incidents were unarmed attempts to rejoin families, recuperate belongings, complete harvests. The Israeli leadership utilized this spontaneous movement of displaced peoples who had lost everything for a campaign to destabilize neighbouring Arab nations and complete the conquest of historic Palestine.[20]

More generally, historians faced the 'Deir Yassin' effect (Deir Yassin was a Palestinian village where locals were massacred by right-wing militias and came to represent a blueprint for Palestinian deportation/depopulation), using evidence that had remained unavailable or unexplored for decades.[21] The accuracy and quantity of the material presented and the detailed analysis of whether each Palestinian village had been deserted as a result of military operations or as a consequence of intimidation make these analyses an invaluable tool for the comprehension of the refugee problem and of Israeli responsibility in its creation. Yet, despite a frank description of atrocities committed against the Palestinian population (from terrorism to expulsion of civilians and outright robbery), Morris, for example, was criticized for not accepting that there was a predetermined plan for the expulsion of the Palestinian population.[22]

A second area of revisionist activity focused on the analysis of Israeli dealings with Arab countries and the role of imperialist powers in the development of these relationships. While this aspect of historical research is not directly connected with the settler/indigenous relationship, these works challenged orthodox understandings of Israel as a polity constantly surrounded by an undifferentiated multiplicity of hostile states.

The theme of collaboration and collusion was crucial in the production of an interpretation that distinguished between different agendas and, at the same time, managed to locate Israeli action in the context of the Arab world. The rigorous separation between the two entities – between the Arab world, on the one hand, and the *Yushuv* (the community of Jews in Palestine before the establishment of the independent state of Israel) and Israel, on the other – was in this way overturned and one important tenet of the historical orthodoxy challenged: there had been a multiplicity of responses to Israeli power and presence. One of the results of this line of research was that the specificity of Palestinian actions was highlighted against a backdrop of contradicting and autonomous agendas pursued by each Arab power. Avi Shlaim's work on the unspoken alliance between Israel and King Abdullah of Jordan is one example of this tendency.[23]

A third strand of revisionist activity has been the progressive exposure of Zionist activity in relation to Nazi persecutions and other 'myths' associated with Zionism. Tom Segev's *The Seventh Million*, for example, illustrated a number of ambiguities in the relation between Nazi authorities during the 1930s and exponents of Zionist organizations.[24] Moreover, his work on the conscious attempt by the Israeli leadership to incorporate the destruction of the European Jewry within the ideological framework of the State of Israel showed how consistent parts of Zionist history and society had been uninvolved in that tragedy.[25] This notion contributed to the creation of a rupture in the history of Zionism, a fissure especially crucial because of one of the 'founding myths' of Israeli society: the notion that the *Yushuv*/Israel was (and had always been) the state of every Jew and not just the expression of one specific political enterprise.

Moreover, as Zeev Sternhell's *The Founding Myths of Israel* – a book also concerned with the political priorities of the leadership of the *Yushuv* – clearly demonstrates, a link can be established between the emergence of Zionism in Palestine and the influence exercised by both Stalin's Russia and National Socialist Germany.[26] His definition of the Zionist project as a type of 'nationalist socialism' represented one high point of a process of historical revision and in a way concluded the process of historical inquiry into the origins of the State of Israel. Sternhell's introduction inscribed the historical experience of Zionism in the long twentieth-century tradition of proto-Fascist movements (of which, in any case, he is one of the most distinguished historians):

> I contend that the inability of the Labor movement under the leadership of its founders and immediate successors to curb aspirations to territorial expansion, as well as its failure to build a more egalitarian society, was not due to any objective conditions or circumstances beyond its control. These developments were the result of a conscious ideological choice made at the beginning and clearly expressed in the doctrine of 'constructive socialism.' Constructive socialism is generally regarded as the Labor movement's great social and ideological achievement, a unique and original product, the outstanding expression of the special needs and conditions of the country. But in reality, far from being unique, constructive socialism was merely an Eretz Israeli version of nationalist socialism.[27]

This claim was obviously received with extreme anxiety in Israel. Not only was the established notion of the irreducible uniqueness of Jewish history here put seriously to the test by a comparative reference to other political experiences of Europe's twentieth century; an authoritative and well-argued allusion to nationalist socialism as an interpretative model for the understanding of Israeli society was inevitably upsetting the very notion of Israel as a response to Jewish persecutions in Europe.

Each of these streams of historiographical activity insisted on the violent and discriminatory character of Israeli history, a violence (and an exclusion) that was not only exercized in the recognized conflicts with its Arab neighbours but was mainly put into effect against an indigenous population whose existence, until the intellectual shifts that began in the 1980s, had not been properly acknowledged.[28] (It should be emphasized, however, that the process of historical revisionism is in many ways incomplete and that, while most 'new' historians have recently argued for notions that Palestinians scholars had already put forward, school textbooks and educational curricula still don't supply in full the historical experience of Palestinians.[29])

And yet the greatest merit of this generation of historians has been to liberate Zionist ideology from the constraints of a single ideological orthodoxy. In the words of Sternhell, the net result of this process has been that

> … the historiographical and sociological debate in Israel in recent years has assumed unprecedented proportions. A distance of some fifty years was needed to examine the relationship of the Yishuv (the Jewish community in Palestine) to the holocaust, the War of Independence, the creation of the problem of Arab refugees, or the social differences in Jewish Palestine with sufficient detachment. These subjects still carry a heavy emotional charge, but they are no longer taboo. Israel is growing up and learning to look at itself and its past.[30]

Unsurprisingly, the most contested ground remains the period between 1947 and 1949, the foundation and consolidation of the State of Israel and its (unilateral) legitimacy *vis-à-vis* Palestinian destruction. In other terms, the collective reception of a comprehensive process of historiographical transformation still needs to attend to the moment of indigenous dispossession: the founding violence of a settler society.

Australian History and Aboriginal History

Until three decades ago a systematic historiography on the experience of Aboriginal people did not exist. Since then, the evolution of the discourses of Aboriginal history has also proceeded along three thematic lines (while dealing with issues quite similar to those distinguishing the 'new' Israeli historiography): the detection of violence, the discovery of Aboriginal collaboration with the pastoral and other industries, and the incorporation of Aboriginal history in the wider context of mainstream Australian historiography. Ultimately, the 'new' Australian history has brought about the denunciation of the genocidal practices that have characterized Aboriginal treatment and policies since the very beginning of the European invasion.[31]

During the 1970s, following a seminal series of Boyer lectures delivered by William Edward Hanley Stanner and his famous denunciation of the 'great Australian silence', Australia witnessed the establishment of 'Aboriginal history' as a recognized field of academic endeavour.[32] What had previously been considered the uncontested domain of anthropologists, ethnologists and archaeologists became an interest of historians too. However, there have been formidable obstacles to the reception of the interpretation proposed by historians and a comprehensively reframed understanding of Australia's past has faced widespread public reluctance. Once established, the myth of 'Aboriginal privilege' has retained its appeal and so has the much older idea that Australia had been exhaustively and peacefully settled. The notion that Aboriginal communities had to endure a generally non-violent process of dispossession is still collectively upheld by wide sectors of the public opinion and, because of the perceived implications this may have on native title, it remains appealing to strong segments of the business community.

During this early historiographical phase, the main interpretative tendency was to highlight European brutality and insist in armed insubordination. This tendency produced a historiography that romanticized Aboriginal resisters while often overlooking Aboriginal agency and objectives. However, the Penguin edition of Henry Reynolds's *The Other Side of the Frontier* became a remarkable editorial success, contributing to popularizing a number of interpretative shifts; it could be seen as concluding the first phase of the rewriting of Aboriginal history: the 'great Australian silence' had been broken.[33] In *The Other Side of the Frontier*, Reynolds summarized a decade of intense research on the dynamics and extent of Aboriginal resistance to European expansion, provided a solid interpretation of Aboriginal resistance and a paradigmatic model of race relations on the Australian frontier. Most importantly, in an attempt to provide an Aboriginal view of the process – the 'other side', the side that had been so systematically neglected in previous historical reconstructions of the conflict – Reynolds systematically initiated the process of incorporating the Aboriginal experience into the 'mainstream' history of Australia.

Throughout the following decade, the interpretation of colonial encounters and conflicts in Australia acquired a marked degree of sophistication and articulation. This line of interpretation stressed the voluntary nature of Aboriginal involvement in both the European world and economic activities.[34] It was not denied that violence and conflict had occurred. However, the new interpretations that were put forward tended to ascribe these issues a significance that was structurally different from previous 'catastrophic' interpretations.[35] 'Violence' played a crucial role in this interpretative approach. In the historiographical tradition established during the 1970s, destructive violence had been the constitutive element of the Australian frontier, its quintessential nature; in that of the 1980s, it was reinterpreted as one result of unequal relations. Colonial relations, it was increasingly argued, developed as a result of consciously made choices and

sometimes even consensual relations: they were not merely
the result of a brutal and inevitably successful imposition of
violent dispossession.[36]

However, a major turning-point in the historical debate and
in public perception was not to come from a history book:
it was the High Court of Australia in 1992 that released the
historic *Mabo* judgment and gave juridical recognition to
the historiographical transformation that had made violent
dispossession a central theme of Australian history.

On the historiographical plane, there were two interrelated
consequences: while this brought into public policy a renewed
history of Australia, it also brought it into collision with
consistent parts of the public opinion. The direct connection
between the High Court decision and the nature of the historical
debate that followed was perceptively described a few years
later by Bain Attwood:

> Mabo and the new Australian history ends the historical silence
> about the Aboriginal pre-colonial and colonial past upon which
> the conservative invention of Australia and Australianness was
> founded, and since their [the conservatives'] Australia was realised
> through and rests upon that conventional historical narrative, the
> end of this history constitutes for them the end of Australia.[37]

The High Court decision itself had a huge impact on the
official and popular self-image of Australia: *terra nullius*,
the notion of an unpossessed country ready for settlement
and appropriation, had been officially rejected. It should be
emphasized that historians had been fully involved in this
process of revision and counter-revision. Indeed, Reynolds's
personal support to Eddie Mabo had been crucial in providing
him with the understanding of the legal issues at stake and
with the motivation to continue a legal battle to have his
entitlements acknowledged and his land returned. Moreover,
The Law of the Land, another book by Reynolds, had been
influential in shaping the climate of opinion that led the Judges
of the High Court to that landmark decision.[38]

In more recent years, failing to face the issue of unsurrendered Aboriginal sovereignty, after a concerted campaign, the debate centred on the allegedly fabricated nature of Australia's renewed historiography.[39] Allegations contesting the very notion of 'stolen generations' (a reference to a long-lasting state-sponsored policy of removing children of Aboriginal descent according to a programme aiming at 'breeding out' the Aboriginal population – a practice that had eventually prompted an official commission of inquiry), for example, or attacking the newly established National Museum for its upsetting inclusiveness of Aboriginal narratives, repeatedly appeared in the press and represented what could be described as a concerted assault on the 'black armband' interpretation of Australian history.[40] The recrudescence of disqualified accepted wisdom is by now an unavoidable fact of Australian intellectual life: then Minister for Aboriginal Affairs Philip Ruddock's remarks on Aboriginal 'incapacity' of developing the wheel and Keith Windschuttle's logic in ruling out settlers' homicidal intentions on the basis of 'Christian beliefs' (and other symptomatically denialist approaches to the question of Aboriginal casualties or the stolen generations) are examples of this tendency.

And yet, it is in this context that the most explicit denunciations of an Australian approach to genocide have come about.[41] As a result, the notion that a colonial genocide was coherently attempted in Australia has been systematically addressed.[42] It is perhaps no coincidence that heated debates coincided with the largest political rally in Australian history on Sydney Bridge in July 2000 – a rally strongly supportive of the reactivation of the process of Aboriginal reconciliation.[43] While the actual content of this 'reconciliation' remained unclear, public opinion on this issue remains strongly divided.

The crucial point is, however, that the very reference to settler violence, or to genocidal practices perpetrated by the administration of the state, brings into question the foundation of the Australian State. Historical reflection on the Aboriginal experience has produced the need for an inevitable reconciliation between what survives of a traditional Australian historical orthodoxy and a history of genocidal violence and erasure from memory. This necessity is epitomized in Reynolds's call for inclusion:

> How, then, do we deal with the Aboriginal dead? White Australians frequently say 'all that' should be forgotten. But it will not be. It cannot be. Black memories are too deeply, too recently scarred. And forgetfulness is a strange prescription coming from a community which has revered the fallen warrior and emblazoned the phrase 'Lest We Forget' on monuments throughout the land. If the Aborigines are to enter our history 'on terms of most perfect equality', as Thomas Mitchell termed it, they will bring their dead with them and expect an honored burial. So our embarrassment is compounded. Do we give up our cherished ceremonies or do we make room for the Aboriginal dead on our memorials, cenotaphs, boards of honor and even in the pantheon of national heroes?[44]

While Reynolds's appeal appeared at the beginning of the 1980s, the most contested grounds remain the issue of casualties on the frontier, and the denunciation of the successive exclusion of Aboriginal people: the acknowledgement of violence in Australia's land wars.[45] In a way that is similar to what happened in Israel, the historical debate is still addressing the moment of indigenous dispossession and expulsion, an erasure based on an explicitly racist rationale: the founding violence of a settler society.

History Writing and Deadlocked Reconciliations

The evolution of these historiographies and the public debates that have surrounded them have proceeded along surprisingly similar lines. In both cases, Aboriginal/Palestinian history moved from erasure to centre stage. Shafir's notion that during 'most of its history, Israeli society is best understood not through the existing, inward-looking, interpretations but rather in terms of the broader context of Israeli-Palestinian relations' is matched by David Day's approach interpreting the whole of Australian national history through the lens of the Aboriginal experience.[46]

Both redescriptions involved the rejection of a pervasive myth of an egalitarian society. And in both cases, exposing this myth in the light of the dispossession of indigenous people and their segregation contributed significantly to intellectual shifts. These parallels are even more striking when one considers the difference between Israel and Australia: the relative absence of violent challenge in the Australian case opposed to the recurring epitome of violence represented by suicidal/homicidal attacks encapsulates this divergence.[47] There are other points of divergence: for example, the internationalization of one conflict opposed to the repeatedly reaffirmed uniqueness of Australian sovereignty (regardless of Aboriginal attempts to involve international organizations to monitor their grievances and regardless of Israeli attempts to prevent any foreign intervention in their dealings with Palestinians), and the mainly repressive nature of Israeli actions against the Palestinian population in contrast with the official rhetoric of a multicultural Australian state.

None the less, despite these obvious chasms, the issues brought about by these historiographical redescriptions – what could be summarized as the discourse on the founding violence – were put on the agenda in comparable ways and have encountered similar public and political rejections. Moreover, these discourses operate in a similar fashion to delegitimize moral claims to an unchallenged sovereignty over their respective polities: it should be noted that both the *Mabo* decision of 1992 and the Oslo Accords/process brought up the issue of Aboriginal and Palestinian sovereignty to their respective publics – a perspective that had, until then, been systematically refused.[48]

The historiographical revision that presupposed, preceded and accompanied both processes of *rapprochement* has, then, operated in two interconnected directions: on the one hand, denouncing the responsibility of the settler polity in the invasion, dispossession and displacement processes, the violence peremptorily used against the indigenous population to enforce balances of power that would be appropriate for the colonizing project; and, on the other hand, highlighting the institutional working of the settler state, a machine used and deployed with all its strength to accelerate the disappearance – cultural, but especially demographic and of course historical – of the indigenous presence.[49] It was a double-pronged and comprehensive reassessment: whereas one strand refers to the history that precedes the establishment of the colonial relation, the other refers to the history that follows that moment.

As noted, despite the revolutionary character of this redescription – or perhaps as a result of it – in both cases the 'new histories' have failed to command public opinion and become accepted wisdom. The difficulties of accepting a revised version of the country's history and the painful process of interiorizing the consequences of this revision, have brought about a situation in which, throughout the 1990s, the politics of a partially reforming settler state lost contact with a historiographical debate that proceeded in a progressively more isolated fashion. The historiographical transformation ultimately backfired in both countries.

Both 'Mabo' and 'Oslo' failed when they came to face the defining question of decolonizing relationships. Despite the intellectual shifts that these processes implied, in both polities, a denial of native title and retention of control over Palestinian territory constituted a major red line for conservative discourses – not only because of the recognition that devolution would demand an intolerable reallocation of resources, but because they would bring to a crisis the founding myths of a society based, essentially, on an invariable denial of indigenous legitimacies to self-determination. In these contexts, manipulating public fears became relatively uncomplicated and a powerful tool of political mobilization.

⟨Permanently relinquishing control over a Palestinian polity and acknowledging native title and self-determination would necessitate disengaging from a state of mind that interprets settler acquisition of land in quasi-mythical and therefore non-negotiable terms.⟩Important sections of the public and political opinion in both countries cling to established local interpretations of *terra nullius*: a condition that forbids the very notion of a negotiated settlement. While *terra nullius* is a relative exception in settler societies, and both 'Mabo' and 'Oslo' have partially denied it, it appears that these settler societies were incapable of reforming their founding mythologies. Departing from *terra nullius* has been easier on paper than in practice and an incapacity of seriously acknowledging indigenous rights, demonstrated by both the Australian native title legislation post-1993 and the transitory status of the arrangements that followed the Oslo Accords, suggest an impasse that goes beyond the political will of conservative administrations. Sharon's definition of the rights of Palestinian Israelis in relation to land – a notion that crucially accepts their presence in the State of Israel but also denies their entitlements – is ultimately very similar to Australian Prime Minister John Howard's notion of 'practical reconciliation' for Aboriginal communities: 'they have every right in the land, no rights to the land'.[50]⟩

In this context, the historical reference to violence, but also, at the other end of the spectrum, the Windschuttlean failure of accepting its reality and Morris's recent rejection of its moral implications, then, emerge in both cases as a crucial site for the production and reproduction of historical and historiographical discourses: a contested ground in the process of redefinition of national identities.[51] For the left, the emergence of the discourses of Aboriginal/Palestinian history has always been connected with the necessity of reappraising the historical record and liberating the interpretation of history from the shackles of what they perceived to be an outdated system of beliefs. However, the production of history is increasingly a strategic arena for the intellectual production of the right too: it is perhaps not a coincidence that former Israeli Prime Minister Binyamin Netanyahu abandoned his portfolio on the eve of the Gaza disengagement, claiming that he needed to feel comfortable with how the history books would portray him, and that Howard has based much of his ascendancy on the awareness of the necessity of 'recapturing' history for the Liberal/National camp.[52] An almost Orwellian necessity of controlling historical production, or at least of contesting left-wing departures from orthodox narratives, has been one important feature of conservative strategies in both Israel and Australia.

The distance between intellectual discourses and public perceptions is not new in Israel, and in many ways is one of the founding characteristics of the original repudiation of traditional Jewry upon which much of Zionism is based. An analogous tendency can be detected in Australia, where a fierce form of anti-intellectualism has always been prominent, and an egalitarian tradition covering noteworthy social differences is exceptionally strong in both countries. Inevitably, the historiographical transition brought about by academic discourse had to contend with a distinctly hostile environment, both at the political level and at the level of the public opinion. In the last analysis, violence as the founding trait of the settler state and community and the consequences that its acknowledgement would inescapably have on the legitimacy of the state epitomizes a sensitive and difficult process.

If an historical investigation on the founding violence of a settler society had obvious reverberations on contemporary contestations, so had scholarly activity facing the historical experience of exclusion of Palestinian and Aboriginal minorities from citizenship rights. In both cases the indigenous population has been subjected to a regime of extraordinary control that was relaxed only at a tantalizingly slow pace (this relates to the experience of Palestinian Israelis – the Palestinians of the Occupied Territories have had no access to citizenship rights). Both indigenous minorities have witnessed a severe limitation of their constitutional rights in a context of strong influx of settler/migrants: while migrants were more or less rapidly absorbed in the context of the settler society, indigenous minorities in both cases were legally and practically excluded from any meaningful participation.[53]

Despite consistent attempts to participate in the institutions of the settler state without abandoning cultural autonomy, both minorities have been incessantly perceived as irreducibly alien to the very nature of the national communities that were developing their colonizing project. While Israel's original constitutional arrangements had provided a framework for the existence of national minorities within its borders, Australia's constitutional practice denied Aboriginal peoples citizenship until 1967. In both cases, the experience of indigenous minorities highlights a situation in which the relationship between foundation myths and historical consciousness remains especially unresolved.

Australian intellectual Ghassan Hage has proposed a very sophisticated analysis of Australia's 'impossible national memory'; his analysis is extraordinarily relevant to Israel/Palestine as well:

> The impossibility of a single Australian national memory or a smoothly plural set of national memories is not the result of there having been a war between two sides, a winning an a losing side. National memories have been forged out of such wars; they are later constructed as 'fratricidal'. As Benedict Anderson argues in the second edition of *Imagined Communities*, there is such a thing as a nationally reassuring memory of fratricide. But this is not possible in Australia today, because the very sides which fought this colonial war have not melted together into one ...
>
> This is the contemporary reality of Australia: two contradictorily located fields of memory and identification. But this is not the

end of the story. For these two sets of memories and identities also mean two communal subjects with two wills over one land; two sovereignties of unequal strength. The first is a dominant one, deriving its legitimacy from the force and the history of its occupation. This is not only the brute force of numbers and technological superiority; it is also the moral force behind a history of inhabiting, transforming and defending the land as it has grown to be. The second is a dominated will, deriving its legitimacy from its historical status as the resisting will of the original inhabitants. One can turn whichever way one likes, but it is as good a definition as any of a colonial situation; a colonial situation that is still with us today.[54]

A long-lasting refusal to seriously address the issue of reconciliation (and possibly sign a 'treaty' that would contribute to a settlement of Aboriginal sovereignty) suggests that the Australian case also displays strong elements of what could be called a 'settler fundamentalism'.[55] Donald Denoon's contention that Australian cultural and political practice had made Australians the faithful representatives of an irredeemably colonialist ideology appears, two decades after its original publication, to be vindicated.[56]

While in both cases an awareness of the necessity of permanently settling these contradictions enjoys wide currency, the political reluctance to act in the inevitable direction of acknowledging violence and redressing exclusion serves as a reminder that the appeal of the colonial project still exercises a strong influence in the discursive production of both countries. Attwood has perceptively stressed the upsetting nature of native title detection in Australia:

> ... the historical changes Mabo portends in the space of Australia challenge a narrative of the nation which has measured its progress relative to an Aboriginal absence or dispossession in that space while simultaneously constructing Aboriginality as the past, and so Aboriginal possession of the land of Australia symbolises for conservatives the end of progress and thus the end of history.[57]

This logic may also apply for the political sectors in Israeli society that contest the very possibility of a peace process which would acknowledge ultimate and meaningful sovereign rights – even if only to the Gaza Strip – to the Palestinians.

Realizing that some areas escaped dispossession and that the colonial project did not and could not succeed to its extreme conclusion, becomes, then, a crucial passage in the process of abandoning a settler lifestyle consciousness, a state of mind that important sections of both societies never abandoned. While it ought to be stressed that this 'settler mentality' is not unique to Israel and Australia, these settler societies remain exceptional in their inability to develop any relevant postcolonial framework of institutional action.[58] In the end, to engage in any sort of postcolonial understanding, one must embrace a vision of history that does not interpret indigenous erasure or absence in terms of 'progress' from an irreducibly detrimental past. These polities share an apparent incapacity, despite the efforts, of distancing themselves from the 'founding violence' that underlies their establishment.

A coherent application of the Oslo Accords would have transformed the Palestine Liberation Organization from an exiled nationalist movement into a sovereign governmental apparatus instated on its territory. On the other hand, the 'treaty' or 'treaties' that have been repeatedly proposed with Aboriginal Australia would enable the shift from a type of sovereignty that is unilaterally affirmed to one that is negotiated and acquires its legitimacy in a shared consensus.[59] It would be an exchange between sovereignty and legitimacy. Australian historian Peter Read recently proposed a swap between 'belonging' (for white Australians) in exchange for an appeasement involving native title. Interestingly, this approach does resonate with the intellectual framework for the establishment of a Palestinian state as delineated in the Oslo process and summarized in the formulation 'land for peace'.[60]

A comparative analysis supports the notion that a post-settler process is particularly difficult in a context where a conspiracy of silence on the 'founding violence' remains hegemonic and where a colonialist project is still operating. While this is apparent when Jewish settlements in the Occupied Territories are expanded and militarily protected, one should note that in the Australian case the idea of assimilation – of assimilation interpreted as a loss of autonomy for Aboriginal communities – is also still present in administrative and political practices. A 'final' settlement is not possible without a strong political commitment, and this is not likely to occur as long as public perceptions are strongly opposed to accepting the idea that the original settlement of European settlers entailed indigenous dispossession and, in the specific circumstances of both an Australian and Zionist colonizations, a negation of indigenous sovereignties. In both cases the state has ultimately failed to become the state of all its citizens but has remained in many ways the state of a colonial project. It does not seem to be an accident that both the postcolonial reorganization of the Australian polity in the early 1990s and the peace process initiated with the Oslo Accords began faltering at the moment of acknowledging indigenous rights to land and self-determination, and at the moment of allowing for a meaningful Palestinian independence.

5

Conclusion: Imperial Engagements and the Negotiation of Israel and Palestine

In French Algeria and apartheid South Africa, it was the shifts in US sensitivities that ultimately produced change, and a similar argument could be made for Australia, since it was the example of the US that, beginning from the late 1960s, created the conditions for an essential shift in public attitudes.[1] Pessimistically, however, one should point out that South Africans had to wait the end of the Cold War before a process of bi-national reconciliation, devolution, and the initiation of a degree of power-sharing. As well, while France negotiated an Algerian independence only after the breakdown of the institutions of the Republic had become irreversible, one should point out that in Australia the Aboriginal reconciliation process remains unfulfilled. Israel/Palestine may need to wait for the end of the permanent global 'war on terror' and/or a full-scale attack on the democratic institutions of the Israeli state before the situation could become unstuck.

In this context, narrative, representation, perception and especially the interpretation of the conflict in the US, become essential.[2] True, contrary to other colonial enterprises, Israel could not count on a colonizing metropole; however, the acceleration of coloniality that accompanied and followed the

87

Oslo process – its current colonial circumstances – is certainly not occurring in a vacuum of empire. Inevitably, an appraisal of Israeli colonial circumstances needs to refer to a re-emerging colonialist sensitivity in the US. A diversion is needed: to negotiate Israel/Palestine, one needs to look at America.[3]

Israel/Palestine and US suburbia are linked. Besides oil, a necessity of 'redesigning' the whole of the Middle East should be interpreted in the light of the extent to which a specific version of settler consciousness has become strategically located in US public and administrative perceptions. 'America's Last Taboo', the unquestioning and automatic US support for Israeli actions in the Occupied Territories, could then be seen as an outcome of a settler consciousness appeased by 'frontier' images of a pioneering enterprise (as well as by the influence exercised by the Zionist lobby on Washington).[4] The pro-Israel lobby is obviously a tremendously influential factor, but, more importantly, one needs to identify the cause of such strength, and move beyond an almost conspiratorial capacity (besides, this approach would risk reproducing overtones of a traditional anti-Semitic stereotyping). A settler-determined constituency and the availability of a settler world-view is one factor that can help explain US support for Israeli policy in the Occupied Territories: the argument of those commentators who insist on the pervasive influence of the pro-Israel lobby in shaping US Middle East policy should be integrated with an appraisal of how crucial the discursive practice of an Israeli settler project has become in the US.[5]

It is the location of a specific settler imagination that should be highlighted: US policy is not biased in favour of Israel because of the pro-Israel lobby; rather, the pro-Israel lobby can be so influential because of a settler-determined consciousness of a specific republican tradition.[6] The paradigmatic shift from a 'peace for autonomy' position to a 'peace for peace' position – from Clinton's 'parameters' to George W. Bush's 'vision' – demands a brand new Middle East. The demographic and military balances of the region also demand it. Surely, the formula 'autonomy yet not sovereignty' plus the chance of opening a gambling outlet in the Jericho 'native reserve' must have sounded familiar to the US Middle East negotiators of the 1990s: 'peace for peace' in the whole of the Middle East, however, necessitated an unprecedented display of imperial force as a basis for peace negotiations.

Indeed, these developments can only be explained if we consider how intertwined US and Israeli perceptions of local and international developments have become.[7] Here are some examples: in October 2004 and in preparation for the presidential elections, US advisers Condoleezza Rice and Richard Holbrooke (respectively National Security Adviser in the Bush Administration and chief foreign policy adviser to Democratic presidential candidate John Kerry) addressed an AIPAC (American Israel Public Affairs Committee) meeting where they presented (very similar) Middle East and Israeli-related policies of their candidates, a type of scrutiny not afforded to other communities.[8] The Global Anti-Semitism Awareness Act, passed by the US Congress in the same month, required the State Department to appoint a special commissioner to keep track of the world-wide evolution of anti-Semitism. The Act was passed despite State Department concerns over the fact that this law confers 'exclusive status' on one specific religion, and treats anti-Semitism differently than other persecutions.[9] Even more explicit: on the eve of his second inauguration, President Bush personally recommended right-wing Israeli politician Natan Sharansky's book, *The Case for Democracy*, as a must-read for those who want an insight on his own and his presidency's world-view.[10] He could certainly choose from an extensive production of US-based conservative opinion, yet he felt most comfortable with a member of the Israeli cabinet.[11]

It is not only an identity of perceptions; the conceptual borderlines dividing Israel and the US have become somewhat blurred. The very fact that during the first George W. Bush Presidency US–Israel relations were conducted primarily by National Security Adviser Rice (and by the Israeli Prime Minister's Office) and not by Secretary of State Colin Powell, as it would appear more appropriate in matters of foreign policy, symbolizes a shift in perception that sees Israeli circumstances as a domestic matter of national security.[12] In an article dealing with the support for Israel of Jewish Americans, and with the 'Franklin affair', where a Pentagon official was accused of having provided classified material to the pro-Israeli lobby AIPAC, *Haaretz* journalist Eliahu Salpeter noted that the 'American Jewish media is at pains to remind those who may have forgotten that in discussing the issue of "dual loyalty," Israel and the United States are not the same country.' Quoting from Jewish-American publication *Jewsweek*, the article reported on a case in which an Israeli citizen was appointed in New Jersey to a state homeland security adviser position despite the fact that as a foreign national he could not receive classified information, and also on the announcement that the former Israeli consul-general in New York was to be appointed as CEO of the American Jewish Congress.[13]

At the same time, besides growing support for an Israeli occupation of the whole of biblical Palestine among fundamentalist Christians in the US, and a consequent identification with the politics of occupation, sections of the same milieus have also attempted a blurring of the distinctions between Christianity and Jewry.[14] On the other hand, shifts taking place in Jewish-American communities seem analogous to changes taking place in the wider community, including the growing number and political activism of religious organizations and Orthodox Jews, as opposed to the traditionally more liberal values of US Jewish constituencies, and an apparent reinforcement of conservative stands. One major result of these transformations is a remarkable coincidence in the narrative and language utilized to discuss terrorism: security-speak in the United States resounds with Israeli usages and informs an increasing number of public domains.[15]

In the end, the political cultures of the two bodies politic have converged and in some strategic aspects have become virtually indistinguishable.[16] This convergence should be related to existing social arrangements and to long-term cultural and political shifts; however, in this context, one should also note that an ideological contiguity between the settlement enterprise in the West Bank and a specific US electoral constituency goes beyond a simple movement of political solidarity. After all, a preference for suburban sprawl and fenced-in properties, as opposed to the *casbahs* of Gaza, Jenin and Nablus – clear examples of the 'dark corners' of Bush's rhetoric – cannot fail to impress and inform American understandings. Of course, this process is not new: already in the 1940s, in a piece entitled 'Palestine Today' *National Geographic* had presented a country that 'is, in a broad sense, the United States of the middle 1800s at the same time that it is, paradoxically enough, California of today'.[17] But this is perhaps more apt now: being at the same time a settler society in its founding moment and a settler society in its current condition allows a powerful degree of identification. Not surprisingly, appeasing settler-related reflexes has been proven to be politically more rewarding than engaging in multilateral actions.[18]

Whereas an instinctive alignment with Israeli world-views could also be related to a Protestant notion that prosperity is a manifestation of grace – and Israeli settlements in the West Bank and Gaza are definitely more prosperous than the Palestinian towns and villages – a capacity for projecting a specific world-view against the conflict in the Occupied Territories is key to understanding US policies.[19] In addition, a constituency's ideological subservience to a settler narrative can be related to the consolidation of a religious sensibility that draws on a specific reading of the Old Testament and Exodus and it is characterized by a somewhat paranoid gaze, obsessed with security, racial profiling, aliens and, after September 11, Arab 'infiltrators'. Most importantly, this constituency's idea of a 'good' community amounts ultimately to a community of religious and individually armed settlers.[20] Under these circumstances, every attack against a settlement in the Occupied Territories amounts to an attack against one of the ideological cores of this constituency.

At times, President Bush's rhetoric is especially attuned with his constituency's: 'There is nothing more deep than recognizing Israel's right to exist, that's the most deep thought of all ... I can't think of anything more deep than that right.'[21] However perplexing initially, this statement actually makes sense if one considers that, contrary to Clinton's aspirations for a postcolonial/neocolonial resolution of sorts in Israel/ Palestine, here Israel's right to exist should be understood as a right to exist *as a settler society*. An enduring contradiction in US policy *vis-à-vis* Gaza and the West Bank should be interpreted in this light. The paradox of officially preventing an annexation of parts or the whole of the Occupied Territories while endorsing and ultimately financing the transfer of settlers and their defence can be finally understood as one result of a political consciousness in which a Jacksonian 'frontier' ethos meets Wilsonian approaches to international legality.

From the point of view of settler colonialism, it is a process that has ultimately come full circle: if it was 'God's American Israel' that was founded by Puritans on Massachusetts Bay, it is God's Israeli America that a specific constituency is seeing founded on the hilltops of the West Bank.[22] 'Redesigning' the Middle East is also one consequence of the successful activation of a settler consciousness in the United States and one legacy of a history of colonial settlement and of the foundational mythologies that relate to it.[23] Facing the intersections and entanglements of Israeli and US colonial traditions and imaginations becomes then a necessary prerequisite in an attempt to mobilize a once strong (and still surviving) anti-colonial and anti-imperial rhetoric.

Whether the Israeli–Palestinian conflict is informed by colonial relations of power is not a merely epistemic issue: the ways in which confrontations are conceptualized, and the systems of reference received narratives are able to deploy, do change the ways in which circumstances are read and solutions are imagined.[24] If the frame of reference remains that of a nationalist conflict between two conflicting bodies politic, including a polity that is not yet established and is perceived as conducting a struggle of national liberation, the visualization of a necessary outcome must include some sort of territorial partition of the geopolitical space. If a nationalist struggle for territory is assumed, one needs to imagine a solution in which nationalist projects of reciprocal ethnic exclusion can be projected onto an undetermined future of national appeasement (or the annihilation of one of the two nationalist projects, as it happened in France/French Algeria/Algeria).

Yet, this partition may not be feasible anymore; possibly as much impracticable as a post-apartheid partition of South Africa could have been. Halper has convincingly demonstrated how a single geopolitical and infrastructural unit has now emerged and how this situation may be irreversible. The transformation of the country and the structures that have been put in place are permanent: what used to be 'two parallel north-south units – Israel and the West Bank, the basis of the two state idea', has been reconfigured 'into one country integrated east-west'.[25] On the contrary, if the paradigmatic system of reference detects a struggle of liberation from a supremacist and largely settler-determined pattern of colonialism, a postcolonial arrangement could imply the establishment of a post-supremacist political system that may acknowledge the self-determination of the colonized within a single political entity (as it could have been for a finally 'reconciled' Australia).

An article by Michael Tarazi, legal adviser to the Palestine Liberation Organization, appeared in the *New York Times* in October 2004 and suggested that a partition of the Israeli/ Palestinian space may not be the best way to approach a resolution of the conflict.[26] Anxious responses to this article appeared in the Israeli press.[27] Barry Rubin's *Jerusalem Post* response concluded that 'the PLO was never a true nationalist movement', that '[h]ad it been, the problem [the Arab–Israeli conflict] would have been solved long ago'.[28] His remark about the defective national character of the Palestinian camp underscores his neglect of the fact that, besides statehood, a Palestinian resistance has also had to face the necessity of expressing an anti-colonial strand. What Rubin sees as 'irrationality from the standpoint of genuine Palestinian nationalism' and just 'another Palestinian mistake' may be the result of a quite complicated situation in which contradictory needs are finding expression.

The Bantustanization that could not be ultimately stabilized through the collaboration of a colonially endorsed Palestinian management had to be unilaterally enforced. A comprehensive policy of separation and control was carried out during the years of the Oslo process; and a wide-ranging policy of separation and destruction was carried out during the years of the Second Intifada – two faces of the same coin. Yet, as insightfully noted by Benvenisti in an article also dedicated to the re-emerging paradigm of a bi-national state as a solution to the conflict, the separation barrier/apartheid wall and the Gaza disengagement plan did not transform the Israeli/Palestinian conflict:

> It is the very processes of unilateral disengagement – the separation fence and the evacuation of the Gaza Strip – that ostensibly are implementing the territorial division of Eretz Israel and distancing the nightmare of a binational state, which in fact are laying the foundations for the binational reality and destroying the option of two states for two peoples. The Israelis believe that the fence turns the conflict into a border dispute, and that disengagement from Gaza alleviates the 'demographic problem'.

However, in effect, the fence and the evacuation create total dependence by defenseless Palestinian cantons. Thus a de facto binational state is being established, which contains many deceptive indicators that enable us to nurture the illusion that it is not such a state, and even to make us feel that the worst of all evils – a binational state – has been prevented. The Palestinians, who correctly understand the significance of the processes – and who are unable to enjoy the luxury of fooling themselves – sense that Israeli activity has in fact made the two-state option impossible, and therefore there must be a return to a one-state strategy.[29]

The widespread impression is that the Israeli–Palestinian conflict is now at a crossroad. As recently summarized in a dispassionate way by respected Israeli historian and commentator Zeev Sternhell, 'the choice is between three options: Israel as a colonialist state that does everything to make the Palestinians' life miserable and to cause them to emigrate, Israel as a Jewish-Arab state in which the Jews will be a minority within a few years or preservation of Israel's present identity on the basis of an overall withdrawal to the Green Line'.[30]

What could probably happen, on the other hand, is a very complicated pattern in which each of these models is tested at the same time in different locales. The institutional imagination of decolonization has been proven a much more flexible way to envisage postcolonial passages than the rigid fixity of nationalist production and imagination. While to negotiate Israel/Palestine one needs to refer to both the specificities of a colonial and imperial contexts, to imagine a postcolonial condition that is both feasible and acceptable to the contending parties, one should perhaps refer *at the same time* to South Africa, to France/Algeria and to Australia. This would possibly be a mix of a 'two states for two peoples' solution and a postcolonial circumstance that would recognize the status of indigenous peoples and their sovereignty in the context of a polity characterized by a balance perceived as largely non-threatening: independence for Gaza, a power-sharing deal based on 'one head one vote' for the remaining Occupied Territories, and a process of national reconciliation within the Green Line.[31] If colonialism can be a suitable interpretative category, the imagination of decolonization can provide guidelines for imagining ways out: what is needed is an Israeli de Gaulle, an Israeli de Klerk and – why not? – an Israeli Paul Keating (the Australian prime minister who initiated the process of Aboriginal reconciliation and was succeeded by another in 1996, who, without proclaiming to do so, progressively discontinued it and reintroduced the politics and logic of an ethnocratic settler society).[32]

There is no easy way out of a colonial situation; closure has always proved elusive and most former colonies maintain vital relations with former colonial powers. Colonialism produces a multiplicity of histories and identities and I am suggesting that a possible negotiation must depart from an appraisal of a multiplicity of colonial histories. After colonialism there is neocolonialism, sometimes a new colonialism, less frequently, a postcolonial disposition: fantasies of a finally resolutive act of unilateral disengagement replicate the logic of colonial imaginings of unilateral and limitless conquest and subjugation.[33] Israelis, Palestinians, Palestinian Israelis and other subjectivities are fated to relate to each other. Instead, parameters for a solution to the confrontation have historically moved back and forth between a one-state solution and a two-state solution.[34] Why must these approaches be exclusive of each other; why not imagine a combination of both?

Until the Palestinian question is dealt with in one way or another – by *rapprochement*, by crushing, by a combination of the two – the current need for a unilateral Bantustanization of Palestinian life will remain. But even a suspension of the conflict or the stabilization of a number of Bantustans will not bring the confrontation to an end.

Notes

Chapter 1 Introduction: Comparing Colonial Conditions

1. See I. Pappe (ed.), *The Israel/Palestine Question*, London and New York: Routledge, 1999. This section is entitled 'The origins of Zionism in Palestine reconsidered' and is comprised of two articles: 'The colonization perspective in Israeli sociology', by Uri Ram, and 'Zionism and colonialism: a comparative approach', by Gershon Shafir (respectively: pp. 55–80, and pp. 81–96). See also D. Stasiulis and N. Yuval-Davis (eds), *Unsettling Settler Societies*, London: Sage Publications, 1995; and C. Elkins and S. Pedersen (eds), *Settler Colonialism in the Twentieth Century: Projects, Practices, Legacies*, London and New York: Routledge, 2005.
2. D. K. Fieldhouse, *Colonialism, 1870–1945: An Introduction*, New York: St. Martin's Press, 1981.
3. A. D. Smith, 'State-Making and Nation-Building', in J. Hall (ed.), *States in History*, Oxford: Blackwell, 1986, p. 241. Smith distinguishes between different patterns of nation-formation: the Western, the immigrant ('where small part-*ethnie* are beneficiaries of a state of their own, with or without a struggle, and they then seek to absorb and assimilate waves of new immigrants from different cultures into what becomes increasingly a territorial nation and a political community, as in America, Argentina, Australia'), the ethnic, and the colonial.
4. See B. Kimmerling, *Zionism and Territory*, Berkeley: University of California Press, 1983; and G. Shafir, *Land, Labor, and the Origins of the Israeli-Palestinian Conflict, 1882–1914*, Cambridge and New York: Cambridge University Press, 1989, p. 10. During the 1970s, Maxime Rodinson had published an analysis of Israel's historical development as a colonial settler state. See M. Rodinson, *Israel: A Colonial Settler State*, New York: Monad Press, 1973. See also Alain Gresh, *Israël-Palestine. Vérités sur un conflit*, Paris: Hachette, 2003. Gresh insists on the eminently colonial nature of the Israeli/Palestinian dispute. A comparative approach with a colonial

dimension is presented in J. Cleary, *Literature, Partition and the Nation-State: Culture and Conflict in Ireland, Israel and Palestine*, Cambridge and New York: Cambridge University Press. For a global analysis of the current relevance of colonial practices, an analysis inclusive of the Palestinian Occupied Territories, see D. Gregory, *The Colonial Present: Afghanistan, Palestine, Iraq*, Malden: Blackwell Publishers, 2004.

5. Historically, the Zionist leadership had explicitly implied an equivalence between Zionism and colonialism. A settler-colonial imprinting associated with Zionism can be gauged, for example, in a 1902 conversation with a member of the Rothschild family reported in Theodor Herzl's diary: 'I moved my chair round to the side of his better ear, and said: "I want to ask the British government for a colonization charter". "Don't say 'charter'. This word has a bad sound", Rothschild replied. "Call it what you please", I replied. "I want to found a Jewish colony in a British possession"', quoted in W. Laqueur, *A History of Zionism*, London: Weidenfeld and Nicolson, 1972, p. 120. For Rothschild, a 'charter' was improper for people who, at best, could aspire to be migrants in someone else's colonial domain and could not be immediately recognized as colonizers. A few generations of Zionist colonial settlement would prove him wrong: Jews could be as good colonists as any. On the colonialist nature of Zionist production in the early decades of the twentieth century, see, for example, M. B. Qumsiyeh, *Sharing the Land of Canaan: Human Rights and the Israeli Palestinian Struggle*, London: Pluto Press, 2004.

6. Both quoted in L. J. Silberstein, *The Postzionism Debates: Knowledge and Power in Israeli Culture*, New York: Routledge, 1999, pp. 109, 227.

7. Quite importantly, the Balfour Declaration of 1917 had identified a Jewish presence not as a settler body but as a migrant one. The inescapable contradiction between two interpretations of a specific colonial enterprise (that is, settler prophecies of domination opposed to an expectation of migrant integration and of a readiness to compromise and submit to an established authority) would eventually precipitate in open conflict between Jewish settlers and British colonialist forces.

8. For an exception to this pattern, see M. N. Barnett (ed.), *Israel in Comparative Perspective: Challenging the Conventional Wisdom*, Albany, NY: SUNY Press, 1996.

9. Y. Marcus, 'Get down from the roof you crazies', *Haaretz*, 05/10/04. (Palestinian madness must be one important feature of Marcus's world-view: a few months later, in a piece commenting on yet another escalation, he presented the same argument and in the

same format: Y. Marcus, 'Get down from the rooftops', *Haaretz*, 19/07/05.

10. Albert Memmi, *The Colonizer and the Colonized*, London: Earthscan, 2003, p. 129. Memmi also notes that 'Another sign of the colonized's depersonalization is what one might call the mark of the plural. The colonized is never characterized in an individual manner; he is entitled only to drown in an anonymous collectivity', ibid.

11. Y. Marcus, 'Get down from the roof you crazies'.

12. F. Fanon, *The Wretched of the Earth*, London: Penguin Books, 1967, p. 31.

13. Jean-Paul Sartre, *Colonialism and Neocolonialism*, London: Routledge, 2001, p. 145. At the same time, Sartre's remark that anti-colonial fighters 'consider themselves potential dead men' is of a striking relevance in an age of suicide bombings and targeted assassinations: 'They will be killed: it is not just that they accept the risk of it, but rather that they are certain of it ... they prefer victory to survival; others will benefit from the victory, not them', ibid., pp. 149–50.

14. This is, alas, something Sartre himself was not willing to do in relation to the Israeli/Palestinian struggle (and the same could be said as regards Memmi). Clearly, even when one is trained in the interpretation of the effects of a colonial relation, it is often very difficult to be sympathetic to someone else's colonization.

15. Ibid. See also A. Mathieu, 'Jean-Paul Sartre et la guerre d'Algérie', *Le Monde Diplomatique*, November 2004, pp. 30–1.

16. D. Levy, 'Coordination is not negotiation', *Haaretz*, 21/01/05.

17. See I. Pappe, 'Fear, Victimhood, Self and Other', *The MIT Electronic Journal of Middle East Studies*, 1, 2001, pp. 4–14.

18. See, for example, A. Harel, 'Dozens of psychologists to help IDF soldiers to cope with Gaza pullout', *Haaretz*, 28/06/05.

19. See, P. Anderson, 'Scurrying towards Bethlehem', *New Left Review*, 10, 2001, pp. 5–30.

20. For examples, see, R. Malley and H. Agha, 'Camp David: The Tragedy of Errors', *The New York Review*, 09/08/01, pp. 59–65; D. Ross, *The Missing Peace: The Inside Story of the Fight for Middle East Peace*, New York: Farrar, Straus and Giroux, 2004, especially pp. 650–771; T. Reinhart, *Israel/Palestine: How to End the War of 1948*, Sydney: Allen & Unwin, 2003, pp. 21–60. For an early review of the literature on the Camp David negotiations of July 2000, see A. Kapeliouk, 'Retour sur les raisons de l'échec de Camp David', *Le Monde Diplomatique*, February 2002, pp. 14–15.

21. K. Ben Simhon 'The outsider', *Haaretz*, 17/09/04. See also O. Shohat, 'Throwing the book at Tali Fahima', *Haaretz*, 31/12/04.

22. Symptomatically, in an *Haaretz* piece Gideon Levy noted how the 'outgoing Shin Bet chief, Avi Dichter, said in one of his farewell interviews that he sees his greatest failure – and apparently the only one in his eyes – in the murder of minister Ze'evi. Not in the murder of about 1,000 Israelis, not in the fear in which the public has had to live for long periods at a time, partly because of his organization's policy of force and killing, but in the single act of murdering a minister', G. Levy, 'The growing gap between the protected and the unprotected', *Haaretz*, 12/06/05.

23. Z. Sternhell, *The Founding Myths of Israel*, Princeton, NJ: Princeton University Press, 1998, p. 345.

24. For contrasting views on the psychology of colonization, see O. Mannoni, *Prospero and Caliban: The Psychology of Colonization*, New York: Praeger, 1964; and F. Fanon, *Black Skin White Masks*, St. Albans: Paladin, 1970.

25. See 'It can happen here', *Haaretz*, 22/11/04.

26. A. Harel, 'Palestinian corpse used for IDF anatomy lesson', *Haaretz*, 28/01/05.

27. See A. Harel, 'Analysis / Reminders of Lebanon', *Haaretz*, 12/05/04, and 'Hamas displays "Israeli remains"', BBC News, 05/12/04. The URL for this article is: <http://news.bbc.co.uk/2/hi/middle_east/3705399.stm>.

28. See E. W. Said, *The End of the Peace Process: Oslo and After*, New York: Pantheon Books, 2000.

29. Said also noted the relevance of Fanon's analysis in colonies where 'imperialism lingers on': 'If I have so often cited Fanon, it is because more dramatically and decisively than anyone, I believe, he expresses the immense cultural shift from the terrain of nationalist independence to the theoretical domain of liberation', E. W. Said, *Culture and Imperialism*, London: Vintage, 1994, pp. 323–4.

30. Ibid., p. 326.

31. See L. Hajjar, *Courting Conflict: The Israeli Military Court System in the West Bank and Gaza*, Berkeley: University of California Press, 2005; and G. Agamben, *Homo Sacer*, Torino: Einaudi, 1995.

32. Of course, the issue of suicide in a colonial context did not emerge in the Occupied Territories of the 1990s. Fanon, for example, noted that on 'the unconscious plane, colonialism therefore did not seek to be considered by the native as a gently loving mother who protects her child from a hostile environment, but rather as a mother who unceasingly restrains her fundamentally perverse offspring from managing to commit suicide and from giving free rein to its evil instincts. The colonial mother protects her child from itself, from its ego, and from its physiology, its biology, and its own unhappiness which is its very essence', F. Fanon, quoted in Said, *Culture and Imperialism*, pp. 286–7.

33. See E. Balibar, 'Universalité de la cause palestinienne', *Le Monde Diplomatique*, May 2004; and L. Galili, 'The devil's own disengagement', *Haaretz*, 06/10/04.
34. See, for example, B. Anderson, *The Spectre of Comparisons: Nationalism, Southeast Asia, and the World*, New York: Verso, 1998.

Chapter 2 The Geography of Unilateral Separation: On Israeli Apartheids

1. For examples, see C. McGeal, 'Anglican group calls for Israel sanctions: Campaigners inspired by boycott of apartheid South Africa', *Guardian*, 24/09/04; N. Guttman, 'A warning signal from the churches', *Haaretz*, 26/11/04, which outlines concerns over calls for the institutions of the Presbyterian Church in the US to divest from Israel as it had happened during the struggle against apartheid South Africa; and H. Eisen, 'At U of T, Arab students' event draws controversy', *Globe and Mail*, 31/01/05, which describes reactions to the organization of an 'Israeli Apartheid Week' event at the University of Toronto.
2. While in February 2005 the World Council of Churches, a global body coordinating non-Catholic Christians, published a call for divestment from Israel and the Anglican Church approved in June 2005 a call for divestment from companies doing business with the Israeli occupation of the West Bank and Gaza, in April 2005 the British Association of University Teachers decided to boycott two Israeli universities (this decision was later reversed). See M. Rapoport, 'Alone on the barricades', *Haaretz*, 06/05/05.
3. See Y. Sheleg, 'From Durban to The Hague', *Haaretz*, 01/03/04.
4. See 'Foreign Ministry warns Israel, Europe on collision course', *Haaretz*, 13/10/04.
5. In May 2005, *Haaretz* commentator Meron Benvenisti noted (and lamented) the increasing recurrence of references to 'apartheid': 'The use of the term apartheid and the comparison between Israel and South Africa under minority white rule are taking over public discourse. In the past week alone, the comparison has been made in at least five instances: the separation fence was described as an "apartheid fence"; the amendment to the Citizenship Law limiting Palestinian family unification was described as worse than the apartheid regime; the academic boycott of Israeli universities and faculty members was compared to the boycott of South Africa, which contributed (or not) to the collapse of apartheid; the disengagement plan and establishment of cantons under Palestinian control were referred to as "bantustans", like the homelands that South Africa

established in the macro-apartheid era; and an academic discussion on the "demographic threat" was accompanied by loud rallies against "racism and apartheid"', M. Benvenisti, 'Apartheid misses the point', *Haaretz*, 19/05/05.

6. E. W. Said, 'The Only Alternative', *ZNet*, 8/03/01. The URL for Said's article is <http://www.zmag.org/sustainers/content/2001–03/08said.htm>.

7. E. W. Said, 'America's Last Taboo', *New Left Review*, 6, 2000, p. 52.

8. Among others, see U. Davis, *Israel: An Apartheid State*, London: Zed Books, 1987; U. Davis, *Apartheid Israel: Possibilities for the Struggle Within*, London: Zed Books, 2003; M. Bishara, *Israel/Palestine: Peace or Apartheid*, London: Zed Books, 2001; and B. Kimmerling, *Politicide: Ariel Sharon's War Against the Palestinians*, New York: Verso, 2003. On the other hand, Norman Finkelstein had explicitly referred to Oslo as 'the apartheid option' already in 1995. See N. G. Finkelstein, *Image and Reality of the Israel–Palestine Conflict*, London, New York: Verso, 1995, pp. 172–83.

9. 'Israeli and Palestinians: Voices from the Frontline', *The Economist*, 21/02/04, p. 23. See also I. Buruma, 'Do not treat Israel like Apartheid South Africa', *Guardian*, 23/07/02.

10. One notable exception in this context is L. Farsakh, 'Israel: An Apartheid State?', *Le Monde Diplomatique*, English edition, November 2003. The URL for this article is <http://mondediplo.com/2003/11/04apartheid>. For other comparative approaches involving Israel and South Africa, see B. Gidron, S. N. Katz and Y. Hasenfeld, *Conflict Resolution in Northern Ireland, South Africa, and Israel/Palestine*, Oxford: Oxford University Press, 2002; and H. Adam, K. Adam and K. Moodley, 'Conditions for Peacemaking: Negotiating the Non-negotiable in South Africa and the Middle East', in U. Schneckener and S. Wolff (eds), *Managing and Settling Ethnic Conflicts*, London: Hurst & Company, 2004. These works, however, do not investigate the colonial character to these conflicts.

11. See T. Keegan, *Colonial South Africa and the Origins of the Racial Order*, London: Leicester University Press, 1996; and Z. Sternhell, *The Founding Myths of Israel*, Princeton, NJ: Princeton University Press, 1998. See also Ilan Pappe (ed.), *The Israel/Palestine Question*, London and New York: Routledge, 1999; and I. Pappe, *A History of Modern Palestine: One Land, Two Peoples*, Cambridge: Cambridge University Press, 2004. Pappe stresses the formative character of the early decades of the conflict.

12. Kimmerling's notion of 'high frontierity' was developed in order to explain Zionist patterns of settler colonization in Israel. According

to this author, the most significant factor in determining settler–indigenous relations is population density, with a high density of indigenous population preventing frontier-like conditions and unchecked dispossession. See B. Kimmerling, *Zionism and Territory*, Berkeley: University of California Press, 1983.

13. A. D. Smith, *Chosen Peoples: Sacred Sources of National Identity*, Oxford, New York: Oxford University Press, 2003, pp. 77–94.

14. Among others, see L. Thompson, *The Political Mythology of Apartheid*, New Haven, CT: Yale University Press, 1985. For a narrative of South African history presenting an analysis of the specificities of the historical geographies of a settler consciousness, see A. Lester, *From Colonization to Democracy: A New Historical Geography of South Africa*, London: Tauris Academic Studies, 1996.

15. 'Transfer' has always been an essential feature of Zionist ideology and has survived decades of political transformations, including the Oslo Accords. See N. Masalha, *Expulsion of the Palestinians: the Concept of 'Transfer' in Zionist Political Thought, 1882–1984*, Washington, DC: Institute of Palestine Studies, 1991.

16. For critical appraisals of these tendencies, see E. Nimni, *The Challenge of Post-Zionism: Alternatives to Fundamentalist Politics in Israel*, London: Zed Books, 2002; and R. Carey and J. Shanin, *The Other Israel: Voices of Refusal and Dissent*, New York: New Press, 2002.

17. See L. Farsakh, 'Israel: An Apartheid State?'

18. Ibid.

19. For example, Israeli historian Zeev Sternhell distinguishes between the two moments of Israeli territorial enlargement: 'Whereas the conquests of 1949 were an essential condition for the founding of Israel, the attempt to retain the conquests of 1967 had a strong flavor of imperial expansion', Sternhell, *The Founding Myths of Israel*, p. 336. However, the 'new' Israeli historiography has highlighted how post-1967 settlements did not represent a deviation of previous Zionist practices. See L. Silberstein, *The Postzionism Debates: Knowledge and Power in Israeli Culture*, New York: Routledge, 1999, p. 122.

20. See G. Shafir, 'Zionism and Colonialism: A Comparative Approach', in Pappe, I. (ed.), *The Israeli/Palestine Question*, London and New York: Routledge, 1999, especially p. 86.

21. See A. Drew, *Discordant Comrades: Identities and Loyalties on the South African Left*, Aldershot: Ashgate, 2000, especially pp. 6–19.

22. See S. Roy, 'Decline and Disfigurement: The Palestinian Economy after Oslo', in R. Carey (ed.), *The New Intifada: Resisting Israel's Apartheid*, London, New York: Verso, 2001, pp. 91–110.

23. See C. Crais, *White Supremacy and Black Resistance in Pre-Industrial South Africa: The Making of the Colonial Order in the Eastern Cape, 1770–1865*, Cambridge: Cambridge University Press, 1992.

24. Quoted in N. Godimer, 'New Introduction', in A. Memmi, *The Colonizer and the Colonized*, London: Earthscan, 2003, p. 30.

25. For an analysis of the legal issues involved in the separate juridical governance of Palestinians of the Occupied Territories and Palestinian Israelis, see B. Kimmerling, 'Jurisdiction in an Immigrant-Settler Society: The "Jewish and Democratic State"', *Comparative Political Studies*, 35, 10, 2002, pp. 1119–44.

26. L. Farsakh, 'Israel: An Apartheid State?'

27. See G. Barzilai, *Politics and Cultures of Legal Identities: Communities and Law*, Ann Arbor: University of Michigan Press, 2003.

28. See S. P. Cohen, M. C. Hudson, N. Guttman and K. E. Jahshan, 'Is a Two-State Solution Still Viable?', *Middle East Policy*, 2, 2003, pp. 1–26; and J. Halper, 'Post-apartheid: One State', UN International Conference on Civil Society in Support of the Palestinian People, New York, 5 September 2003. The URL for this article is <http://www.fromoccupiedpalestine.org/node.php?id=772>.

29. On this question, and in respect of the international context, Farsakh emphasises the differences between South Africa and Israel/Palestine: 'The international community never accepted apartheid or the idea of separate nationhood in South Africa ... In the Israeli–Palestinian conflict, the UN endorsed separate nation states as the model for conflict resolution. The UN Security Council resolution 181 in 1947 clearly set up the idea of land-for-peace as the guiding principle for solving the conflict. UN Security Council resolution 242 in 1967 reaffirmed that principle. While not specific about the boundaries of the land that Israel occupied or about Palestinian national rights, resolution 242 affirmed that the way to peace in the Middle East had to be through returning land and recognising all states. The Oslo process was based on resolution 242', Farsakh, 'Israel: An Apartheid State?'

30. For analyses of the influence of shifting US attitudes *vis-à-vis* the South African apartheid regime, see C. Coker, *The United States and South Africa, 1968–1985: Constructive Engagement and its Critics*, Durham, NC: Duke University Press, 1986; and P. N. Lyman, *Partner to History: the U.S. Role in South Africa's Transition to Democracy*, Washington, DC: United States Institute of Peace Press, 2002.

31. Said, 'America's Last Taboo', p. 52.
32. Farsakh, 'Israel: An Apartheid State?' For other examples of this approach, see also N. Guyatt, *The Absence of Peace: Understanding the Israel–Palestinian Conflict*, London: Zed Books, 1998; R. Carey (ed.), *The New Intifada: Resisting Israel's Apartheid*, London and New York: Verso, 2001; and Reporters Without Borders, *Israel/Palestine: The Black Book*, London: Pluto Press, 2003.
33. A. D. Smith, 'State-Making and Nation-Building', in J. A. Hall (ed.), *States in History*, Oxford: Basil Blackwell, 1986, p. 242.
34. A. Eldar, 'People and Politics/Sharon's Bantustans are far from Copenhagen's hope', *Haaretz*, 14/05/03.
35. Quoted in B. Kimmerling, 'From Barak to the Road Map', *New Left Review*, 23, 2003, p. 143.
36. 'The Disengagement Plan of Prime Minister Ariel Sharon', *Haaretz*, 01/04/04.
37. In a long interview with *Haaretz* journalist Ari Shavit, Dov Weisglass, a close collaborator of Sharon, further clarified that the Gaza Disengagement Plan is designed with the explicit intention of forever postponing the peace process, any peace process, and rerouting international pressure on Israel. See A. Shavit, 'The big freeze', *Haaretz*, 08/10/04. On the other hand, in preparing for the implementation of the pullout from Gaza, Israeli officials have proposed creating ambiguous definitions regarding the status of a vacated Gaza still under Israeli military control: 'a step toward ending the occupation', a flexible definition of 'effective control of the area', declaring that the Oslo Accords 'are still valid and that the disengagement is a withdrawal in the framework of one of the "phases" of that accord'. Aluf Benn noted that 'Israel would like to receive international legitimacy for the claim that the occupation will end with the disengagement; but international law does not recognize any interim conditions and only speaks of occupation or lack of occupation', A. Benn, 'Israel talks with UN, U.S. on post-pullout status of territories', *Haaretz*, 22/11/04.
38. Israeli academic and commentator Tanya Reinhart has stressed the substantial concurrence of the policies pursued by the two Prime Ministers and the unprecedented role of the military in producing this consensus. See T. Reinhart, *Israel/Palestine: How to End the War of 1948*, Sydney: Allen & Unwin, 2003, pp. 78–87, 198–207. On the role of the military, see also B. Kimmerling, *The Invention and Decline of Israeliness: State, Society, and the Military*, Berkeley: University of California Press, 2001.
39. For an analysis of these legislative structures (Bantu Authorities Act 1951, Promotion of Bantu Self-Government Act 1959, Bantu

Homeland Citizenship Act 1970), see L. Thompson, *A History of South Africa*, New Haven, CT: Yale University Press, 2001.

40. For examples, see Guyatt, *The Absence of Peace*; and J. Halper, '*Nishul* (Displacement): Israel's form of Apartheid', Institute of African Studies, School of International and Public Affairs, Columbia University, 20/09/02. The URL for this article is <http://www.columbia.edu/cu/sipa/REGIONAL/IAS/documents/apartheid.doc>.

41. Even right-wing National Union Party leader Avigdor Lieberman, for example, stated at the 2004 Herziliya conference that he supported a transfer to Palestinian control (yet not to a Palestinian state) of areas, including parts of Jerusalem, currently under unilaterally declared Israeli sovereignty (this, according to his perception that Israel's primary problem is its Arab citizens and not 'the Palestinians'). See L. Galili, 'Lieberman: Transfer Arab areas of Jerusalem to Palestinians', *Haaretz*, 17/12/04.

42. It should be noted that the issue of language and, specifically, the question of an education in English for South African blacks was one contested issue during the apartheid era. On the politics of language in the Middle East, see Y. Suleiman, *A War of Words: Language and Conflict in the Middle East*, Cambridge: Cambridge University Press, 2004.

43. Significantly, segments of the Israeli-Palestinian community have also shown a tendency towards withdrawing from participation in the wider political processes. See Oren Yiftachel, '"Ethnocracy": The politics of Judaizing Israel/Palestine', *Constellations*, 6, 3, 1999, pp 364–90; and O. Yiftachel, 'The Shrinking Space of Citizenship: Ethnocratic Politics in Israel', *Middle East Report*, 223, 2002. The URL for this article is <http://www.merip.org/mer/mer223/223_yiftachel.html>. Yiftachel stresses the necessity of interpreting Israeli politics in a way that allows for an increasing degree of ethnocratic discrimination.

44. M. Benvenisti, 'Democracy, but not here', *Haaretz*, 02/12/04.

45. See Y. Laor, 'Referendum means apartheid', *Haaretz*, 03/02/05.

46. See, for example, M. Rapoport, 'Amour, guerre, démographie', *Le Monde Diplomatique*, February 2004, p. 15. This legislation was extended again in 2004 and early 2005. A January 2005 *Haaretz* editorial detected a crucial shift from citizenship to a (colonially determined) stratification of statuses and commented that 'It should be hoped that it's not only up to the Shin Bet to decide who will fall in love with Israeli citizens and with whom Israeli citizens will be allowed to marry and start a household. The Citizenship Law in its old form allowed the state to examine closely every immigrant and anyone who wanted to settle here ... The citizenship tests for non-

Jews were always strict, but the new law cancels all the tests and prefers a sweeping, disproportional denial of citizenship to Arabs from outside the country, 'Racist legislation', *Haaretz*, 18/01/05.

47. As director of Adalah, Hasan Jabarin, noted, the outcome of the changes to the Citizenship Law approved in May 2005 is a stratification of citizenship rights for different citizens of the state of Israel: 'The amendment to the Citizenship and Entry into Israel Law – which was approved this week in the cabinet – creates three separate ethnic tracks for citizenship in Israel: a track for Jews, a track for Arabs and a track for 'foreigners' ... Supporters of the amendment, including prominent members of the academic world, claim that every country is permitted to determine its immigration policy. That is true, but first of all, we are not talking about immigration, but about granting legal status to the partner of a citizen. Second, there is no democratic country in the world that restricts immigration on the basis of ethnicity. Third, the ethnic component – the "Arab" component in our case – is the identity component of 20 per cent of all the citizens of the State of Israel, and therefore, such a step has the power to grant open and official legitimization for discrimination against Arab citizens, in all areas.' See H. Jabarin, 'From discrimination to the denial of basic freedoms', *Haaretz*, 18/05/05. Adalah is a centre for the protection of Israeli Arabs' legal rights.

48. See E. W. Said, 'Palestinians Under Siege', *London Review of Books*, 14/12/00. The URL for this article is <http://www.lrb.co.uk/v22/n24/said01_.html>.

49. Silberstein, *The Postzionism Debates*, especially Chapter 1, pp. 15–46.

50. Said, 'Palestinians Under Siege'.

51. An insightful analysis of the 'matrix' is available at the Internet site of the Israeli Committee Against House Demolitions. See J. Halper, 'The Key to Peace: Dismantling the Matrix of Control', ICAHD. The URL for this article is <http://www.icahd.org/eng/articles>.

52. See M. Benvenisti, 'The Illusion of Soft Borders', *Haaretz*, 14/10/99, also quoted in Roy, 'Decline and Disfigurement', pp. 101–2.

53. The necessity of moving beyond a two-dimensional geography and appraising the occupation in its 'volumetric' aspects is argued by Eyal Weizman in a perceptive essay entitled 'The Politics of Verticality', *openDemocracy*, 30/01/2003. See also J. Elmer, 'Israel and the Empire: Jeff Halper interview', *FromOccupiedpalestine. org*, 20/09/03. The URL for this article is <http://www. fromoccupiedpalestine.org/index.php?or=64>.

54. See J. Robinson, *The Power of Apartheid: State, Power, and Space in South African Cities*, Oxford and Boston, MA: Butterworth-Heinemann, 1995.

55. See, for example, E. W. Said, *The End of the Peace Process: Oslo and After*, New York: Pantheon Books, 2000. With regards to the formation of collaborationist elites in the post-Oslo Occupied Territories, Fanon's analysis of the division and contradiction between the nationalist bourgeoisie in Algeria and the FLN's liberationist tendencies – a contradiction that involves conflicting narratives – can be an insightful departure. See F. Fanon, *The Wretched of the Earth*, London: Penguin Books, 1967, especially pp. 46–50, and 119–65.

56. Quoted in Said, *The End of the Peace Process*.

57. An insightful analysis of the background to the policy of deporting foreign workers is presented in J. Singh, 'The Tel Aviv suicide bombing and illegal foreign workers', *The Electronic Intifada*, 07/01/03. The URL for this article is <http://electronicintifada.net/cgi-bin/artman/exec/view.cgi/7/1041>.

58. 'Israel will examine, together with Egypt [but of course not with a Palestinian counterpart], the possibility of establishing a joint industrial zone on the border of the Gaza Strip, Egypt and Israel', 'The Disengagement Plan of Prime Minister Ariel Sharon'.

59. See M. Rapoport, 'A l'ombre du mur, Israël construit des zones industrielles', *Le Monde Diplomatique*, June 2004, pp. 16–17.

60. See A. Harel, 'Analysis/Not the Last Attempt', *Haaretz*, 07/03/04.

61. Quoted in Y. Laor, 'Diary', *London Review of Books*, 03/10/02. The URL for this article is <http://www.lrb.co.uk/v24/n19/laor01_.html>.

62. Ibid.

63. For example, see E. Inbar, 'The End of the Palestinian Option', *Haaretz*, 23/03/04. This piece proclaims that 'There is a sick society living alongside the State of Israel that is lead by a pathological national movement', and that 'There is no reason to assume that if poverty were replaced by plenty Palestinian desires would be abated', etc. The author of this collection of medicalizing insights on Palestinian politics and society is professor of political science at Bar-Ilan University, and director of the Begin-Sadat Center for Strategic Studies.

64. See J. Halper, 'The 94 Percent Solution: A Matrix of Control', *Middle East Report*, 216, 2000.

65. For example, see J. Halper, 'The Three Jerusalems', ICAHD, 06/01/01.

66. D. Gregory, *The Colonial Present: Afghanistan, Palestine, Iraq*, Malden: Blackwell Publishers, 2004, p. 252.

67. Strategies of mobility control deployed against Palestinian mobility may not be limited to the segregation applying on a number of roads. Recent analyses of traffic lights positioning in Eastern Jerusalem highlight how, in a context where there are almost no traffic lights at all, stoplights are placed only where there is a 'Jewish' traffic flow. In this case, time allotted for the different traffic flows is decided on an ethnic rationale, creating long lines of vehicles waiting for access at intersections with 'Arab' roads. See D. Rubinstein, 'The Battle for the capital', *Haaretz*, 31/03/05, which refers to the work of Betselem researcher Karim Jubran.

68. On the 'architecture' of the occupation and the geography it employs, see E. Weizman, 'The Geometry of Occupation', *openDemocracy*, 9/09/03, 10/09/03, 15/09/03.

69. A sophisticated analysis of the changing significance of the Green Line during the 1990s is presented in A. S. Bornstein, *Crossing the Green Line between the West Bank and Israel*, Philadelphia: University of Pennsylvania Press, 2002.

70. Y. Laor, 'Al-mahsum, mahsom, checkpoint', *Haaretz*, 02/12/04.

71. See A. Hass, 'The Wall: Palestinians Now "Illegal Residents"; IDF redefines Palestinians West of the Fence', *Haaretz*, 14/10/03.

72. A. Hass, 'Qalandiyah in the rain', *Haaretz*, 24/11/04.

73. D. Tutu, 'Apartheid in the Holy Land', *Guardian*, 29/04/02.

Chapter 3 The Troubles of Decolonization: France/Algeria, Israel/Palestine

1. On the 'unmixing of peoples' see, for example, R. Brubaker, 'Aftermaths of Empire and the Unmixing of Peoples', in R. Brubaker, *Nationalism Reframed: Nationhood and the National Question in the New Europe*, Cambridge: Cambridge University Press, 1996, pp. 148–78.

2. H. Keinon, 'Some Precedents', *Jerusalem Post*, 08/05/03.

3. See J. Halper, 'The 94 Percent Solution: A Matrix of Control'. As well, one should note that the Algerian Front de Libération Nationale called France the 'Seventh Wilaya' (area of operations, the other six were Algeria) and that the history of participation of Algerian workers in France to the independence struggle is a very complicated one. See A. Haroun, *La 7e Wilaya: La Guerre de FLN en France, 1854–1962*, Paris: Seuil, 1986.

4. For example – but this reference is an amazingly recurrent one – see Y. Alpher, 'Hard Questions, Tough Answers: A weekly APN Q & A with Yossi Alpher June 2, 2003', Americans for Peace Now, 02/06/03; the URL for this article is: <http://www.peacenow.org/nia/briefs/QA060203.html>. See also H. Siegman, 'Sharon's Phony

War', *New York Review of Books*, 18/12/03, p. 16; and A. Tal, 'For the left, Sharon will always be Sharon', *Haaretz*, 26/08/04.

5. *Haaretz* commentator Yoel Marcus also approached the Sharon/de Gaulle refrain: 'I don't think there is a single other country in the world in which, from morning to evening, so many ministers are prepared to be interviewed on any subject under the sun and by all the media, banging state secrets back and forth like they were ping-pong balls. The worst comes with holiday interviews, especially those given by the top dogs. Sharon gave seven interviews over the holidays. The interviewers, some politely and others brashly, tried to extract a scoop, but Sharon wouldn't budge from a predetermined text that was basically empty of content. President Charles de Gaulle used to give two news conferences a year. Reporters were briefed on what to ask and de Gaulle, using a key he had been given, knew exactly who to take questions from. And then one day, there was a snag. The news conference ended and one of the questions hadn't been asked. After a minute of uncomfortable silence, de Gaulle said: "I think I heard a question that I haven't answered yet, and the following is my response." That was the day he described Israelis as "an elitist people, self-assured and domineering" – a few words that ended the special relationship between the two countries', Y. Marcus, 'Six comments on the situation', *Haaretz*, 01/10/04.

6. See I. S. Lustik, *Unsettled States, Disputed Lands: Britain & Ireland, France & Algeria, Israel & the West Bank/Gaza*, Ithaca, NY: Cornell University Press, 1993; U. Dromi, 'Illuminating the dark alleys of decolonization', *Haaretz*, 17/07/02, which reviews for an Israeli public a spate of recent publications relating to the Algerian war of independence, and R. Miran, 'Nothing new under the sun', *Haaretz*, 24/09/04, which reviews the Hebrew translation of M. S. Alexander, M. Evans and J. F. V. Keiger (eds), *The Algerian War and the French Army, 1954–62: Experiences, Images, Testimonies*, London: Palgrave Macmillan, 2002. See also G. Merom, *How Democracies Lose Small Wars: State, Society, and the Failures of France in Algeria, Israel in Lebanon, and the United States in Vietnam*, Cambridge and New York: Cambridge University Press, 2003. Although it involves a sustained comparison between Israel and French Algeria, this work does not address the West Bank and Gaza. Finally, see Tony Judt, 'Israel's Road to Nowhere', *New York Review of Books*, 09/05/02, pp. 4–6. Judt's piece explicitly refers to French philosopher Raymond Aron's 1958 examination of French entanglements in Algeria and his insightful proposition that French settlers had to leave the country. R. Aron, *L'Algérie et la République*, Paris: Plon, 1958. Aron's call for abandoning Algeria was translated into Hebrew and published by *Yedioth Ahronoth* in

2005 as a contribution to the discussion concerning the evacuation of settlements from Gaza.

7. On the Algerian war, see, for example, J. Frémeaux, *La France et l'Algérie en guerre: 1830–1870, 1954–1962*, Commission Française d'Histoire Militaire/Institut de stratégie comparée: Paris, 2002; A. Clayton, *The French Wars of Decolonization*, Longman: London, 1994; J. P. Vittori, *On a torturé en Algérie*, Paris: Ramsay, 2000; and A. Horne, *A Savage War of Peace: Algeria 1954–1962*, London: Pan, 2002.

8. *Haaretz* commentator Gideon Samet also suggested that the transition to the Fifth Republic on the basis of territorial compromise could be a model of institutional transition for Israel, G. Samet, 'On to the Fifth Republic', *Haaretz*, 31/12/04.

9. For examples, see I. M. Wall, *France, the United States and the Algerian War*, Berkeley: University of California Press, 2002; and C. G. Cogan, 'France, the United States and the Invisible Algerian Outcome', *Journal of Strategic Studies*, 25, 2, 2002, pp. 138–58.

10. See K. Ross, *Fast Cars, Clean Bodies: Decolonisation and the Reordering of French Culture*, Cambridge, MA: MIT Press, 1996.

11. On the evolution of Palestinian nationalism see, for example, R. Khalidi, *Palestinian Identity: The Construction of Modern National Consciousness*, New York: Columbia University Press, 1997; N. Masalha, *Imperial Israel and the Palestinians*, London: Pluto Press, 2000; and B. Kimmerling and J. S. Migda, *The Palestinian People: A History*, Cambridge, MA: Harvard University Press, 2003.

12. R. Pedatzur, 'More than a million bullets', *Haaretz*, 29/06/04. See also I. Laor, 'Diary', *London Review of Books*, 03/10/02.

13. See, for example, R. Fisk, 'In on the tide, the guns and rockets that fuel this fight', *Independent*, 29/04/02.

14. See M. Arens, 'They fought for the country', *Haaretz*, 21/12/04. The distinction between fighting 'for the country' and fighting 'for *their* country' epitomizes the colonial character of these colonial auxiliaries' participation in the Israeli military effort.

15. Y. Ettinger, 'Druze torn in their relationship with state', *Haaretz*, 19/12/04. The June 2005 conviction of an IDF soldier of the Bedouin Reconnaissance Battalion for the killing of a British citizen in Rafah in 2003 epitomizes the entanglements of a racially constructed situation: in this case, it was an exceptional situation in which a non-Palestinian victim had been killed by a non-Jewish Israeli soldier, A. Harel and Y. Yoaz, 'IDF soldier convicted of manslaughter of British activist', *Haaretz*, 28/06/05.

16. On the experience of Algerian military personnel in the French army during the war in Algeria, see, for example, Frémeaux, *La France et l'Algérie en guerre*, especially pp. 139–42.

17. J.-P. Sartre, *Colonialism and Neocolonialism*, London: Routledge, 2001, pp. 96–119. While a collected edition of these articles was originally published in 1964, an English translation of this volume has only recently been published.

18. See ibid., especially pp. 54–135. In *How Israel Lost*, Pulitzer Prize winner Richard Ben Cramer argues that Israel is being slowly destroyed by the continued occupation of the West Bank and Gaza, which is in turn destroying Palestinian hopes for an independent homeland. See R. B. Cramer, *How Israel Lost: The Four Questions*, New York: Simon & Schuster, 2004.

19. Sartre, *Colonialism and Neocolonialism*, pp. 45, 147.

20. See Clayton, *The French Wars of Decolonization*, p. 166; and C. McGeal, 'We're air force pilots, not mafia. We don't take revenge', *Guardian*, 03/12/03. The public letter of the Air Force pilots, one remarkable exception to a generalized climate of public apathy, is available, for example, at the Internet site of the Foundation for Middle East Peace. 'Pilots' Letter', Foundation for Middle East Peace, October 2003. The URL for this letter is <http://www.fmep.org/analysis/PilotsLetter10–2003.html>.

21. For example: 'Disturbing reports have emerged recently of doubts among IDF chiefs about the disengagement operation assigned to them and their role in evacuating settlers. According to a *Haaretz* report, '[In] a select forum with the prime minister the IDF expressed the opinion that "ensuring an orderly democratic process" is important to the success of the evacuation operation ... It is fair to assume that the IDF opinion at such a high-level gathering was uttered by the Chief of Staff, Moshe Yaalon. If that is so, he was speaking out of turn in the established hierarchy between the military and civil authorities. He who is so concerned about harming the orderly democratic process during the disengagement must be all the more sensitive to the serious mistake of involving the military leadership in the process itself', 'The brass must be quiet', *Haaretz*, 26/09/04.

22. While Yaalon commented that 'it will take more than a division to repair the trouble created by withdrawing from one settlement under fire', Sharon's response was to point out that the lieutenant general was blatantly intervening in political matters. See A. Benn, 'PM summons chief of staff to clarify his criticism of pullout', *Haaretz*, 09/03/04. Yaalon's appointment would be discontinued after the final approval of the disengagement from Gaza. On the opposition between army and political leaders, see Yaalon's interview in *Haaretz*, A. Shavit, 'Parting shots', *Haaretz*, 02/06/05.

23. Gideon Levy, for example, reminded *Haaretz* readers in February 2005 that the 'Israeli Defense Force must disengage from the settlers now. This process of disengagement will be difficult – the IDF is deeply invested in the settlement enterprise – but it is obligated by reality. Even before a single settler family is evacuated, the army must untie its Gordian knot with the settlers, which has bound it for many years. The time has come for it to again be the Israeli Defense Force, as intended, rather than the Settler Defense Forces, as it has been throughout the long years of occupation', G. Levy, 'No border between Yesha and the IDF', *Haaretz*, 06/02/05. On defiance in the IDF, see also M. Rapoport, 'The orange battalion', *Haaretz*, 14/07/05.

24. See, for example, M. van Creveld, *The Sword and the Olive: A Critical History of the Israeli Defense Force*, New York: Public Affairs, 1998.

25. Sartre, *Colonialism and Neocolonialism*, pp. 104–5.

26. Clayton, *The French Wars of Decolonization*, p. 169.

27. Quite interestingly, a number of Israeli commentators have constructed settler opposition to the prospected evacuation as a slide towards Palestinian political behaviour, reproducing a classic theme of colonial settings, where anxieties regarding the possibility of 'going native' traditionally enjoy a broad currency:

> Radical youths hurl rocks, metal objects and fists at soldiers, swarm onto their backs and spit in their faces.
>
> The protesters, many of them young women and children, invoke Scripture in vowing to lay down their lives in defense of sites they hold sacred.
>
> Denouncing soldiers as Nazis, the protesters demand the immediate withdrawal of all Israeli troops and security forces from the area.
>
> An IDF paratrooper, believing to have seen one of the demonstrators draw a handgun, fires a warning shot into the air.
>
> From the pulpit, bearded sages urge escalation in active resistance to Israeli governmental and military policies.
>
> The aging veteran leaders of the movement wring their hands, saying the youths are now beyond their control, and holding Israel's leaders squarely responsible for all bloodshed that may ensue.
>
> A growing number of soldiers, reservists, and high schoolers on the verge of conscription, sign petitions pledging to refuse orders concerning service in the territories.

B. Burston, 'Background/The 3rd Intifada: Settlers take on their own Army', *Haaretz*, 06/01/05.

28. Veteran left-wing politician Yossi Sarid polemically noted the existence of an autonomous 'Rhodesian' settler polity besides Israel: 'Perhaps out of an oppressive sense of regional isolation, or perhaps out of the suffocating distress of being surrounded, the State of Israel decided 38 years ago to establish a friendly state alongside itself: This was "the state of Judea", which had its beginnings in a Jewish settlers' restaurant in Hebron and eventually spread to the northern tip of Samaria (the West Bank). The neighboring countries – Israel and Judea – were originally intended as two states for one nation, but as time passed it became clear that in fact two states arose for two nations here: the nation of the Jewish settlers and the nation of Israel, and the similarity between them dwindled. It is quite possible that the founding fathers and others – Golda Meir and Yisrael Galili and Moshe Dayan and Shimon Peres (now vice-premier) and Yigal Allon and Ariel Sharon (now prime minister) and Menachem Begin – meant to set up a protectorate state, which the government in Jerusalem ran in actuality. But we quickly learned that the state of Judea was "seizing independence" and was run according to laws and values of its own', Y. Sarid, 'Sorry, my stock of pain has run out', *Haaretz*, 24/01/05. On the other hand, a typically colonial dreamtime can be detected in military historian and Gaza Strip settler Dr Aryeh Yitzhaki's description of relations with Palestinian neighbours: 'We lived among thousands of Arab with no fear. The Arabs call the place "The Tel of the Two Demons"; they were frightened of us. When the Arabs made trouble and harassed our visitors on the road, we made it clear to them that if they continue, we will banish them back to Khan Yunis where they came from', N. Hasson, 'Extremists resorting to scare tactics against disengagement', *Haaretz*, 17/01/05.

29. While a group of rabbis has explicitly called for violence in the Occupied Territories even if it is known that innocents will be killed in an attack, calls on soldiers to disobey evacuation orders were also authoritatively and repeatedly put on the agenda. See 'The dangers of the rabbis' declaration', *Haaretz*, 09/09/04, and 'Toward the edge of the abyss', *Haaretz*, 19/07/05, which comments on a call by two former chief rabbis for soldiers to refuse obeying the military order to prevent pull-out opponents from entering the Gaza Strip. In a completely different context, the Harvard Law School held a conference in October 2004 on the possible evacuation of settlers from areas of the West Bank and Gaza. Among several other issues, including 'a psychological base for the call to a more empathetic debate in Israel over the future of the settlements', a panel reflected on some 'hard lessons drawn from the cases of the French experience in Algeria'. See Program on Negotiation, Harvard

Law School, 'Negotiation Conference Examines West Bank and Gaza Settlements', 21/10/04. The URL for this article is <http://www.pon.harvard.edu/news/2004/conference_settlers.php3>.

30. A. Shavit, 'Ready to cross lines', *Haaretz*, 19/07/05.
31. For an authoritative appraisal of the limitations of military success in the Algerian war, see Frémeaux, *La France et l'Algérie en guerre*, pp. 295–300.
32. B. Burston, 'Background/Sharon's do-or-die Gaza plan – or is it do AND die?', *Haaretz*, 11/03/04.
33. Shavit, 'Parting shots'. One should note that Yaalon here was recalling a determination to prove that terrorism does not pay *before* the militarization of Palestinian resistance.
34. Ibid.
35. Ibid.
36. In *Courting Conflict* Lisa Hajjar perceptively noted that a major dissimilarity between the First and Second Intifadas can be determined in an extensive and generalized suspension of legal procedure, an evolution that can be ascertained in the Algerian war as well. On a shift towards an abandonment of the pretence of a legal order in the two contexts, see L. Hajjar, *Courting Conflict: The Israeli Military Court System in the West Bank and Gaza*, Berkeley: University of California Press, 2005, and S. Thénault, *Une drôle de justice. Les magistrates dans la guerre d'Algérie*, Paris: La Découverte, 2001.
37. In June 2005, *Maariv* documented an episode in which an IDF unit was given explicit orders to carry out untargeted killings. The IDF did not dispute this report. See 'When everything is possible', *Haaretz*, 06/06/05.
38. See, for example, M. Benvenisti, 'What lies at the bottom of the barrel', *Haaretz*, 12/08/04.
39. 'The routine of death', *Haaretz*, 09/03/04.
40. Indeed, one could detect a parallel genealogy in the development of French and Israeli anti-insurgency approaches in Algeria and in the Occupied Territories. Military historian Anthony Clayton's assessment of the lessons that were drawn from the conclusion of the Indochina campaign could apply to IDF appraisals of the lessons to be drawn from the end of the occupation of Southern Lebanon: 'But the general conclusion drawn [from the conclusion of the Indochina campaign] by many French officers was that in a conflict of this type, the efforts of the entire nation, and not simply cadres of regular officers NCOs, must be committed; and that a new combat doctrine of a total war against revolutionary movements must be developed. The psychological warfare staffs were especially blamed for failure in this respect. Both these conclusions and the general feeling that

"it must not happen again" were to have disastrous consequences in France's next major colonial campaign, Algeria, before the lesson was finally learnt that social and nationalist challenges cannot be crushed by technical solutions', Clayton, *The French Wars of Decolonization*, p. 76.

41. A shared assumption of the two strategies is an unshakeable conviction that every military challenge can be appropriately met with a technical solution. *Haaretz* correspondent Reuven Pedatzur has expressed concerns in relation to this expectation: 'Telling the truth and making it clear that not every threat has a military-technological solution requires leadership and civil courage. Regrettably, those qualities are not in abundant evidence among senior figures in the defense establishment. It is sad to discover that after four years of fighting in the territories the defense establishment is in a state of conceptual stagnation. Nothing demonstrates better what has happened to the shapers of our defense policy than the very idea of investing tens of millions of dollars in developing a defensive system against metal pipes that are manufactured on home lathes', R. Pedatzur, 'Pipe dreams', *Haaretz*, 17/10/04.

42. See also T. Roger, *Modern Warfare; a French View of Counter-insurgency*, New York: Praeger, 1964.

43. Clayton, *The French Wars of Decolonization*, pp. 129–30. A comprehensive doctrine of *Riposte* had been developed in Algeria by French military theorists. It could be summarized in ten points; each of them also noticeably resonating with Israeli strategy *vis-à-vis* the Occupied Territories: '1) no equal terms negotiations with insurgents; 2) the isolation of rebel-held territory; 3) early pre-emptive security force action; 4) an infrastructure that linked all civil, military, political and social work; 5) the destruction of insurgent hierarchies; 6) a psychological campaign to convince the population that the insurgents were false and that improved living standards would follow the restoration of law and order; 7) recognition that the destruction of the insurgents was not enough in itself; 8) that insurgent groups should be stifled by deprivation of material and moral support; 9) that the insurgents themselves should be harassed and tracked ceaselessly; and 10) that key installations should not be secured by static defence but by constant insecurity for any attacker'. See ibid., pp. 130–1.

44. On 'counter-terrorism' as it was practised by the French army in Algeria, see the controversial and autobiographical volume by P. Aussaresses, *The Battle of the Casbah: Terrorism and Counter-terrorism in Algeria, 1955–1957*, New York: Enigma Books, 2002. General Aussaresses commanded intelligence operations during the Battle of Algiers; his unrestrained recollection, where he confessed to

be a murderer and a torturer, constituted undoubtedly a publishing success and was translated into English and published in the US at a time when there was a growing public interest in the delivery of torture to 'terrorists' and in the technologies of counter-insurgency in an urban and Arab setting. On the same subject see also R. Branche, *La Torture et l'armée pendant la guerre d'Algérie*, Paris: Gallimard, 2001; and Thénault, *Une drôle de justice*; both are recent works that effectively address the legacy of French 'counter-insurgency' actions in Algeria. In the case of Israel's war 'on terror', see, for example, A. Shavit, 'He took terror to task', *Haaretz*, 15/09/04.

45. R. Malley and H. Agha, 'The Last Palestinian', *New York Review of Books*, 50, 2, 10/02/05, p. 14.

46. See D. Rivet, *Le Maghreb à l'épreuve de la colonisation*, Paris: Hachette, 2002, pp. 412–13.

47. Clayton, *The French Wars of Decolonization*, p. 141.

48. See Siegman, 'Sharon's Phony War', p. 16.

49. For examples, see U. Benziman, 'Victors beware', *Haaretz*, 26/09/04; A. Harel, 'One Friday afternoon four years ago', *Haaretz*, 12/09/04; and B. Burston, 'Background: The war that Palestine couldn't lose – and did', *Haaretz*, 01/10/04.

50. See C. Krauthammer, 'Israel's Intifada Victory', *Washington Post*, 18/06/04.

51. *Haaretz* commentator Uzi Benziman proposed a different interpretation: 'In other words, the armed Palestinian uprising has [had] a real effect on the decision to withdraw. The difference between Netanyahu and Ariel Sharon is that the former continues to deny the facts of life while the latter explains that today he sees things that he did not see yesterday. Even if the finance minister and Israeli Defense Force heads continue claiming that Israel has won, or warning not to present things in a way that the Palestinians would perceive as their success, the verbal make-up would not cover the scars of reality. The Palestinian guerrilla war is indeed about to drive Israel out of the entire Gaza Strip and a part of northern Samaria. The mighty IDF and the rest of the advanced security branches, with all their abundant resources, failed to subdue the Palestinian rebellion', U. Benziman, 'So sorry we didn't win', *Haaretz*, 08/05/05.

52. See A. Benn, 'Tactical victory, strategic debacle', *Haaretz*, 14/07/04.

53. K. Toolis, 'You can't make a deal with the dead', *Guardian*, 10/09/03.

54. A. Oren, 'The defense minister's responsibility', *Haaretz*, 12/05/04. See also A. Oren, 'Rewriting history is easy', *Haaretz*, 01/06/04.

55. While the use of targeted assassinations and incursions can be used in the attempt to shape (Palestinian) historical understandings, the Israeli army – which has a unique and traditionally very active historical unit and publishing house – has fought other historiographical battles with more traditional but not less determined methods. Teddy Katz was a Masters student whose work dealt with the events between 22 and 23 May 1948 in Tantura, a Palestinian village near Haifa, when approximately two hundred Palestinians were massacred after they had surrendered. His thesis, based on oral sources (of both Israeli military and Palestinian survivors), was originally accepted, but, after loud protests emanating from the military, reconsidered (some of the former IDF personnel interviewed claimed they had been cheated). Katz was threatened, accused and forced to abjure his research (he claimed he had been forced to do so under duress). His appeal to have his work rehabilitated was turned down by the judiciary. For an outline of the 'Katz affair', as a result of which well-known Israeli historian Ilan Pappe has been threatened with expulsion from his university, see I. Pappe, 'The Tantura Case in Israel: The Katz Research and Trial', *Journal of Palestine Studies*, 30, 3, 2001, pp. 19–39.

56. The Israeli Defense Force Archive (a civil institution that is operated by the Defense Ministry and is part of the Israeli State Archives) selectively grants the status of 'authorized researcher', which accords access to documents and to the archives, and traditionally supervises the scope and content of historical research. See A. Dayan, 'How did Jewish settlements begin? It's a secret', *Haaretz*, 29/03/05.

57. See E. W. Said, *Culture and Imperialism*, London: Vintage, 1994, p. xiii.

58. E. W. Said, 'Palestinians under Siege', *London Review of Books*, 14/12/00.

59. Surveys highlight how the percentage of Palestinians who view Sharon's disengagement plan as victory for the armed Intifada has increased from 66 per cent in March 2004 to 74 per cent in September 2004. This proportion was confirmed in a more recent poll (March 2005), which noted that 'Three quarters of the [Palestinian] public view, as the case has been during the past year, the Israeli disengagement plan as a victory for armed struggle.' See 'Survey Research Unit: Public Opinion Poll # 13', Palestinian Center for Policy and Survey Research, 23–26/09/04; and 'Survey Research Unit: Public Opinion Poll # 15'. The URL for these surveys are <http://www.pcpsr.org/survey/polls/2004/p13a.html>, and <http://www.pcpsr.org/survey/polls/2005/p15a.html>.

60. D. Rubinstein, 'The Palestinian "crossing"', *Haaretz*, 31/01/05. This proposition assumes (in a rather Orientalizing way) that Arabs

would generally be unable to approach rationally a negotiation process but could only settle for peace after a specific sensibility has been appeased. Of course, this perspective could also be reversed, and one could note how it is a specific colonial sensibility that allows withdrawal from occupied territory (that is, from Sinai and from Lebanon) only after what can be construed as a military failure.

61. F. Fanon, quoted in Said, *Culture and Imperialism*, p. 327.
62. Ibid.
63. F. Fanon, *The Wretched of the Earth*, quoted in ibid.
64. See Z. Segal, 'Strengthening freedom of speech', *Haaretz*, 07/09/04. After a number of legal actions, in September 2004, the Israeli Supreme Court allowed public screenings of Mohammed Bakri's movie.
65. D. A. Low, 'The Contraction of England: An Inaugural Lecture, 1984', in D. A. Low, *Eclipse of Empire*, Cambridge: Cambridge University Press, 1991, pp. 1–21.
66. On the history of French decolonization, see, for example, T. Chafer, *The End of Empire in French West Africa: France's Successful Decolonization?*, Oxford: Berg, 2002.
67. See R. B. Betts, *Assimilation and Association in French Colonial Theory, 1890–1914*, New York: Columbia University Press, 1961; and A. L. Conklin, *A Mission to Civilize: The Republican Idea of Empire in France and West Africa, 1895–1930*, Stanford, CA: Stanford University Press, 1998.
68. Quoted in D. Little, *American Orientalism: The United States and the Middle East since 1945*, London and New York: I. B. Tauris, 2002, p. 277.
69. Doron Rosenblum commented insightfully on this colonial schizophrenia and on a typically associated pedagogical drive in a January 2005 piece: 'Breaking off contact in the wake of a terror attack, as well as preparing for another major military operation, as well as conducting talks; both withdrawal and annexation; both despairing of the Palestinians and continuing to etch their awareness; disengaging unilaterally, because there is no partner, as well as waiting for that partner to die, as well as trying to educate him; both withdrawal because of the blood price, and declaring that there will be no disengagement under fire, in order to show who's the boss here, etc. etc. ... but the Palestinian student is apparently hard to educate. Thousands of shells have not etched his awareness; 100 "gestures" have not shaken him up; and in spite of the Sisyphean pedagogical process, in which Israel is breaking stick after stick on the back of the Palestinians, or is waving carrot after carrot in front of them in an effort to reshape them, they insist on being Arabs rather than members of the Mistaravim [Israeli undercover

units who disguise themselves as Arabs]'. He concluded calling for 'cutting the pedagogical Gordian knot', a good description as any of a decolonized situation, D. Rosenblum, 'The chaos is working', *Haaretz*, 21/01/05.

70. Meron Rapoport noted that the fact that Israeli voters have had to go to the polls four times in less than seven years between 1996 and 2003 – 'a record in the Western world' – can be interpreted as 'a symptom of profound illness', a 'malady [that] might be called the virus of indecision'. In his article, Rapoport refers to the fact that in France 'between World War II and the rise of Charles de Gaulle to the presidency in 1958, more than 50 governments came and went, to a large extent because of the war in Algeria', M. Rapoport, 'The Israel election virus', *Haaretz*, 06/12/04.

71. Quoted in Rivet, *Le Maghreb à l'épreuve de la colonisation*, p. 414.

72. 'It's a complex story, Gush Katif [an evacuated Gaza settlement]. On the one hand, it is indeed Algeria. Distinctly Algeria. a baseless settlement project of a mother-state that chose to place a low-income population in occupied territory. A closed local regime that maintains a colonialist farm economy, nourished by cheap land, cheap water and cheap labor, all originating in the military occupation', A. Shavit, 'Chronicle of an end foretold', *Haaretz*, 19/08/05.

Chapter 4 Founding Violence and Settler Societies: Rewriting History in Israel and Australia

1. Ross, *The Missing Peace: The Inside Story of the Fight for Middle East Peace*, New York: Farrar, Straus and Giroux, 2004, chapter 1.

2. On this specific point, Fanon penetratingly linked the settler's conquest of history with imperialism's regime of truth, over which the great myths of a settler colonial consciousness preside: 'The settler makes history; his life is an epoch, an Odyssey. He is the absolute beginning. "This land was created by us"; he is the unceasing cause: "If we leave all is lost, and the country will go back to the Middle Ages". Over against him torpid creatures, wasted by fevers, obsessed by ancestral customs, form an almost inorganic background for the innovating dynamism of colonial mercantilism', F. Fanon, quoted in E. W. Said, *Culture and Imperialism*, London, Vintage, 1994, pp. 323–4.

3. While conducting research on the comparative historiography of Israel and Australia, I submitted early drafts of my work to two friends – one Australian and one Jewish-Italian. Both agreed that I

could not suggest a moral equivalence between the two cases. One noted that since 1966, Australian governments have transferred title over 18 per cent of the Australian land mass to indigenous Australians and that it is plausible that this quantity will grow. He suggested also that in Australia there is a debate about the price that indigenous people have paid in being colonized and noted that there is no immediate Israeli equivalent for this debate. Conversely, my Italian friend emphasized that atrocities and discrimination (in Israel/Palestine) do not equal extermination and colonial genocide (in Australia). Paradoxically, they concurred: Rafah is not Redfern (an inner-city Sydney suburb where there is a strong community of indigenous Australians). However, it is unclear whether it would be better to be a Palestinian refugee in the former or a dispossessed Aboriginal Australian in the latter. Yet again, New South Wales premier Bob Carr wanted Redfern bulldozed.

4. For an authoritative example, see W. Laqueur, *A History of Zionism*.

5. Quoted in Little, *American Orientalism*, p. 300.

6. See B. Attwood, 'A Tour of Duty in Australia's History Wars', *Australian Financial Review*, 01/06/2001; and S. Macintyre and A. Clark, *The History Wars*, Melbourne: Melbourne University Press, 2003.

7. G. Hage, *Against Paranoid Nationalism: Searching for Hope in a Shrinking Society*, Sydney: Pluto Press, 2003, p. 48. Perhaps it is not an accident that the July 2004 United Nations General Assembly's motion on the 'separation fence' – a motion that followed an International Court of Justice's non-binding ruling based on the Fourth Geneva Convention – was supported by an overwhelming majority of 150 against the votes of settler nations who have not enacted yet a postcolonial/post-settler passage: Israel, Australia, the United States (and three of its Pacific dependencies). See L. Veracini, 'The Fourth Geneva Convention and its Relevance for Settler Nations, Including Australia', *Arena Magazine*, forthcoming.

8. R. Brunton, 'Genocide, the "Stolen Generations", and the "unconceived generations", *Quadrant*, May 1998. See also Human Rights and Equal Opportunity Commission, *Bringing Them Home, Report of the National Inquiry Into the Separation of Aboriginal and Torres Strait Islander Children from their Families*, Canberra, Commonwealth Printer, 1996; and C. Bird (ed.), *The Stolen Children: Their Stories*, Sydney: Random House, 1998.

9. For the Australian case, see K. Neumann, N. Thomas and H. Ericksen (eds), *Quicksands: Foundational Histories in Australia and Aotearoa New Zealand*, Sydney: University of New South Wales

Press, 1999; for an overview of the Israeli case, see, for example, G. Piterberg, 'Erasures', *New Left Review*, 10, 2001.

10. While in the Australian debate, Ray Evans insisted on the notion of 'indigenocide' as one way of approaching the Aboriginal experience, in an Israeli context, Kimmerling has formulated 'politicide' as one definition of Israeli policies towards Palestinians. These are understandably loaded terms: yet, this terminology may indicate that, in one case, the political activism of Aboriginal Australians is discounted while, in the other case, it is the indigenous character of Palestinian resistance that is ignored. Of course, there was a lot of political agency informing Aboriginal resistances while, conversely, Palestinian resistances cannot be collapsed and exhausted in its politics. See R. Evans and B. Thorpe, 'Indigenocide and the Massacre of Aboriginal History', *Overland*, 163, 2001, pp. 21–39, and B. Kimmerling, *Politicide: Ariel Sharon's War Against the Palestinians*, New York: Verso, 2003.

11. See, for example, C. Choo and S. Hollbach (eds), *History and Native Title*, Perth: University of Western Australia Press, 2003.

12. See, for example, N. Caplan, 'The "New Historians"', *Journal of Palestine Studies*, XXIV, 4, 1995, pp. 96–103; E. Karsh, *Fabricating Israeli History: The 'New Historians'*, London: Frank Cass, 1997 (whose discourse and title would be reproduced in a remarkably similar fashion by Keith Windschuttle), and B. Morris, 'Refabricating 1948', *Journal of Palestine Studies*, XXVII, 2, 1998, pp. 81–95.

13. Y. Porath, *The Emergence of the Palestinian-Arab National Movement: 1918–1929*, London: Cass, 1974.

14. Australian Labor leader Gough Whitlam's victory in 1972 may have produced a comparable dynamic in breaking a long-lasting and consolidated political regime and creating a climate more receptive of innovative historical research.

15. A discussion of this theme is contained in G. N. Arad (ed.), *Israeli Historiography Revisited*, special issue of *History and Memory*, 7, 1, 1995. See also D. Vidal, *Le Péché originel d'Israel. L'expulsion des Palestiniens revisité par les 'noveaux historiens' israéliens*, Paris: Atélier, 1998.

16. Of course, history was only one site of academic disputation. Sociology, for example, became another especially contested ground. See L. J. Silberstein, *The Postzionism Debates: Knowledge and Power in Israeli Culture*, New York: Routledge, 1999, pp. 11–113; and U. Ram, *The Changing Agenda of Israeli Sociology: Theory, Ideology, and Identity*, Albany: SUNY Press, 1995.

17. See R. Sayigh, *Too Many Enemies: The Palestinian Experience in Lebanon*, London: Zed Press, 1994; N. H. Aruri (ed.), *Palestinian Refugees: The Right of Return*, London: Pluto Press, 2001; and

K. Christison, *The Wound of Dispossession: Telling the Palestinian Story*, Santa Fe, NM: Sunlit Hills Press, 2001.

18. B. Morris, *The Birth of the Palestinian Refugee Problem, 1947–1949*, Cambridge: Cambridge University Press, 1987; and B. Morris, *1948 and After: Israel and the Palestinians*, New York: Oxford University Press, 1990. It should be noted, however, that one consequence of the Second Intifada was Morris's 'conversion' to an uncompromising approach in relation to Palestinian demands. See A. Shavit, 'Survival of the Fittest? An Interview with Benny Morris', *Haaretz*, 01/09/03.

19. It should be said, though, that – possibly as a result of a process of exclusion from the official historical record – refugees have always managed to preserve an exceptionally intact collective tradition of the *Nakba* of 1948–49 ('catastrophe' – the expulsion from land and homes). For a sophisticated analysis of the mechanisms of Palestinian remembrance and, conversely, the strategies deployed by the Israeli establishment in order to terminate the sites of Palestinian historical memory, see Piterberg, 'Erasures'. For an analysis of the legal and extralegal technologies of dispossession, see M. R. Fischbach, *Records of Dispossession: Palestinian Refugee Property and the Arab-Israeli Conflict*, New York: Columbia University Press, 2003.

20. See B. Morris, *Israel's Border Wars, 1949–1956: Arab Infiltration, Israeli Retaliation, and the Countdown to the Suez War*, New York: Oxford University Press, 1997.

21. See also I. Pappe, *The Making of the Arab-Israeli Conflict, 1947–51*, London, New York: I. B. Tauris, 1992.

22. Nur Masalha, *Expulsion of the Palestinians: The Concept of Transfer in Zionist Political Thought, 1882–1984*, Washington, DC: Institute of Palestine Studies, 1991. Masalha insists on population transfer as a paradigm for the founding of the Israeli state and proposes an interpretation that is only partially compatible with Morris's: there was no need for a plan because the very foundation of Israel was the plan. If one acknowledges that the deportation of Palestinians was organized and carried out in a piecemeal fashion and with the least publicity possible, the question of whether a plan for Palestinian deportation had been executed becomes, therefore, much less relevant. This is similar to Aboriginal approaches to frontier violence: there is no proof of organized genocide because the very process of invasion, dispossession and displacement is proof of a genocidal intent. On the issue of genocidal intent in a settler context, see A. D. Moses, 'Genocide and Settler Society in Australian History', in A. D. Moses (ed.), *Genocide and Settler Society: Frontier*

Violence and Stolen Indigenous Children in Australian History, New York: Berghahn Books, 2004, pp. 3–48.

23. See A. Shlaim, *Collusion Across the Jordan: King Abdullah, the Zionist Movement and the Partition of Palestine*, Oxford: Clarendon Press, 1988.

24. See T. Segev, *The Seventh Million: The Israelis and the Holocaust*, New York: Hill & Wang, 1993. See also T. Segev, *1949: The First Israelis*, New York: Free Press, 1986.

25. T. Segev, *C'était en Palestine au temps des coquelicots*, Paris: Levi, 2000.

26. Z. Sternhell, *The Founding Myths of Israel*, Princeton, NJ: Princeton University Press, 1998.

27. Ibid., p. 6.

28. Conversely, the historical orthodoxy of the Zionist left had always rejected the idea that violence had been the fundamental feature of the Israeli experience and had always insisted either on the relative 'emptiness' of the Zionist frontier, on the legality of the acquisition of land for Zionist use and settlement, and on an extraordinarily humane and progressive process of settlement guided by the 'purity' of Zionist intentions.

29. See, for example, A. Eldar, 'Learning all the wrong facts', *Haaretz*, 09/12/04.

30. Sternhell, *The Founding Myths of Israel*, p. x.

31. See L. Veracini, 'Of a Contested Ground and an Indelible Stain: The Difficult Reconciliation between Australia and its Aboriginal History during the 1990s and 2000s', *Aboriginal History*, 27, 2003, pp. 226–41; and A. Haebich, 'The Battlefields of Aboriginal History', in M. Lyons and P. Russell (eds), *Australia's History: Themes and Debates*, Sydney: University of New South Wales Press, 2005, pp. 1–21.

32. W. E. H. Stanner, *After the Dreaming*, Sydney: Australian Broadcasting Commission, 1968. For an excellent review of 'Aboriginality', both in the European and the Australian discourses from the early phase of contact to the 1920s, see the still unsurpassed article written in the early 1960s by D. J. Mulvaney, 'The Australian Aborigines, 1606–1929; Opinion and Fieldwork', Part 1 and Part 2, in J. J. Eastwood and F. B. Smith (eds), *Historical Studies: Selected Articles*, Melbourne: Melbourne University Press, 1964, pp. 1–56.

33. See H. Reynolds, *The Other Side of the Frontier: Aboriginal Resistance to the European Invasion of Australia*, Melbourne: Penguin, 1982.

34. For examples of this interpretative trend, see A. McGrath, *'Born in the Cattle': Aborigines in Cattle Country*, Sydney: Allen & Unwin, 1987; M. Fels, *Good Men and True: The Aboriginal Police*

of the Port Phillip District, 1837–1853, Melbourne: Melbourne University Press, 1988; H. Reynolds, With the White People, Melbourne: Penguin, 1990; D. May, Aboriginal Labour and the Cattle Industry: Queensland from White Settlement to Present, Melbourne: Cambridge University Press, 1994.

35. See R. Broome, 'Aboriginal Victims and Voyagers, Confronting Frontier Myths', Journal of Australian Studies, 42, 1994, pp. 70–77.

36. See H. Goodall, Invasion to Embassy: Land in Aboriginal Politics in New South Wales, 1770–1972, Sydney: Allen & Unwin, 1996.

37. B. Attwood, 'Mabo, Australia and the end of History', in B. Attwood (ed.), In the Age of Mabo: History, Aborigines and Australia, Sydney: Allen and Unwin, 1996, p. 116. It should be noted that a very similar argument could be made in relation to the Oslo process and conservative politics in Israel. In this case, the officially endorsed recognition of Palestinian rights to an independent state (at least in a future perspective) upset the historical vision of a Jewish state established on the whole of Israel. For a brief outline of the contrasting technologies of memory developed in an Israeli context, see U. Ram, 'There's a time and place for them', Haaretz, 14/06/03.

38. See N. Loos, Edward Koiki Mabo: His Life and Struggle for Land Rights, Brisbane: University of Queensland Press, 1996; and H. Reynolds, The Law of the Land, Melbourne: Penguin, 1987.

39. See K. Windschuttle, The Fabrication of Australian History, Vol. 1: Van Dieman's Land, 1803–1847, Sydney: Macleay Press, 2002; and R. Manne (ed.), Whitewash: On Keith Windschuttle's Fabrication of Aboriginal History, Melbourne: Black Inc., 2003.

40. The conservative journal Quadrant initially proposed these themes in a series of articles by Keith Windschuttle, who stressed the 'impossibility' of generalized frontier violence. He rejected decades of historical research with a self-fulfilling assumption: the British were civilized and could not do barbaric things; they did not perform massacres because they were civilized. Here is an example: 'There is one good, general reason why we should expect the eventual compilation of regional studies to produce a very much smaller tally of violent Aboriginal deaths than the 20,000 now claimed [by Reynolds]. Ever since they were founded in 1788, the British colonies in Australia were civilised societies governed by both morality and laws that forbade the killing of the innocent. The notion that the frontier was a place where white men could kill blacks with impunity ignores the powerful cultural and legal prohibitions on such action. For a start, most colonists were Christians to whom such actions were abhorrent. But even

those whose consciences would not have been troubled knew it was against the law to murder human beings, Aborigines included, and the penalty was death' K. Windschuttle, 'The Break-Up of Australia', *Quadrant*, September, October and November 2000. For rejoinders to Windschuttle's attacks, see R. Manne, *In Denial: the Stolen Generation and the Right*, Melbourne: Black Inc., 2001; and Manne, *Whitewash*. See also B. Attwood, *Telling the Truth about Aboriginal History*, Sydney: Allen & Unwin, 2005.

41. See A. Haebich, *Broken Circles: Fragmenting Indigenous Families, 1800–2000*, Fremantle: Fremantle Arts Centre Press, 2000.

42. On colonial genocide in an Australian context, see H. Reynolds, *An Indelible Stain? The Question of Genocide in Australia's History*, Melbourne: Penguin, 2001; A. Curthoys and J. Docker (eds), *'Genocide'?: Australian Aboriginal History in international perspective*, special issue of *Aboriginal History*, volume 25, 2001; and Moses, 'Genocide and Settler Society in Australian History'.

43. On 'Aboriginal Reconciliation', see M. Grattan (ed.), *Essays in Australian Reconciliation*, Melbourne: Bookman Press, 2000.

44. Reynolds, *The Other Side of the Frontier*, p. 201.

45. On Australia's 'land wars', see B. Attwood and S. G. Foster (eds), *Frontier Conflict: The Australian Experience*, Canberra: National Museum of Australia, 2003.

46. G. Shafir, *Land, Labor, and the Origins of the Israeli-Palestinian Conflict, 1882–1914*, Cambridge and New York: Cambridge University Press, p. xi; and D. Day, *Claiming a Continent: A New History of Australia*, Sydney: HarperCollins, 2001.

47. This point deserves an exploratory note. Albeit in completely different forms and ideological contexts, self-destructive practices are apparent in both Aboriginal and Palestinian behaviour: in the case of Palestinian resistance, political agency is recognized (and acted upon with anti-insurgency violence) while the damage brought about by a colonial regime is disregarded; in the other case, the destruction of Aboriginal society is acknowledged (and acted upon, through an intervention at the level of welfare) while indigenous agency is in many ways still aggressively rejected. In both cases one witnesses a misreading based on the incapacity/unwillingness of appraising *at the same time* the effects of a devastating colonial regime and the survival of indigenous agency. In one case, the indigenous presence that precedes the establishment of the colonial regime is erased and conceptually replaced with absence; in the other case, the autonomy that survives the establishment of the colonial regime is denied. Acknowledging Palestinian destruction would demand reconsidering an ethnocratic settlement enterprise, recognizing Aboriginal agency would require allowing for Aboriginal

self-determination. Neither conservative opinion is apparently willing to perform this exercise.

48. David Day's *Claiming a Continent* is a recent overview of Australian history that repeatedly insists on the fragility of both claims to the continent, the original British one and that of today's non-indigenous Australia, a claim that, as long as the issue of Aboriginal sovereignty is not settled, descends directly from its predecessor. See Day, *Claiming a Continent*. In this respect, it is noteworthy that the settler societies that have evolved differently in their relationship with their moral legitimacy are apparently better off. For example, Labour Prime Minister of Aotearoa/New Zealand Helen Clark could confide to the readers of *The Australian Women's Weekly* in November 2001: 'I think you [Australians] feel more insecure [even though] I think you should be secure and confident in what you are and who you are. I think New Zealand often appears to the rest of the world to be more secure, confident and independent than Australia', 'Interview with Helen Clark', *The Australian Women's Weekly*, November 2001, p. 56.

49. In this respect, the experiences of Australia and Israel diverge in a marked way. While the permanence of Aboriginal names on the Australian landscape is indicative of a colonial state of mind that is conscious of conquest as a *fait accompli*, in the Israeli case, the need for a complete reformation of the geographical nomenclature may denote a far less secure claim. On the other hand, it is indicative that in the anxious age of Prime Minister John Howard, very rarely do the new suburban developments display Aboriginal names. For analyses of the intersections between archaeology and current confrontations, see K. W. Whitelam, *The Invention of Ancient Israel: The Silencing of Palestinian History*, London: Routledge, 1996; and E. Fox, *Palestine Twilight: Murder and Malice in the Holy Land*, Sydney: HarperCollins Australia, 2002.

50. Quoted in A. Benn and Y. Verter, 'Even King Solomon ceded territories', *Haaretz*, 22/04/05.

51. Interestingly, both Morris and Windschuttle present themselves as 'positivist' historians who apprehensively disdain 'political correctness'. Not only the public has been reluctant to receive a renewed historiography, in their case, it is the historian who is reluctant to digest his own work – possibly one result of a 'psychopathology of colonialism'. See Shavit, 'Survival of the Fittest?'; G. Ash, 'Diagnosing Benny Morris; the mind of a European settler', *YellowTimes.org*, 24/01/04 (the URL for this article is <http://www.yellowtimes.org/article.php?sid=1750>); and B. Kimmerling, 'Benny Morris's Shocking Interview', *History News Network*, 26/01/04 (the URL for this article is <http://hnn.us/articles/3166.html>). It is also

interesting to note that Windschuttle's blend of anti-postmodernism and attacks against a more inclusive historiography resonate with Israeli debates assessing the relationship between post-Zionism and postmodernity. Despite this attacks, it should be noted how both the new Australian and the 'new' Israeli historiographies have presented mainly research carried out according to quite traditional methodologies. K. Windschuttle, *The Killing of History: How a Discipline is being Murdered by Literary Critics and Social Theorists*, Sydney: Macleay Press, 1994; and Silberstein, *The Postzionism Debates*, pp. 124–6.

52. See also S. Brawley, 'A Comfortable and Relaxed Past: John Howard and the "Battle of History" The First Phase – February 1992 to March 1996', *The Electronic Journal of Australian and New Zealand History*, 1, 1996. The URL for this article is <http://www.jcu.edu.au/aff/history/articles/brawley.htm>.

53. See, for examples, J. Chesterman and B. Galligan, *Citizens Without Rights: Aborigines and Australian Citizenship*, Melbourne: Cambridge University Press, 1997; and T. Rowse, 'Indigenous Citizenship' in W. Hudson and J. Kane (eds), *Rethinking Australian Citizenship*, Melbourne: Cambridge University Press, 2000.

54. Hage, *Against Paranoid Nationalism*, pp. 92–4. See also B. Anderson, *Imagined Communities: Reflections on the Origin and Spread of Nationalism*, London, New York: Verso, 1991.

55. The result of the 2001 Federal election may have been determined also by John Howard's refusal to proceed on the road of reconciliation, as opposed to Labor's commitment to a formal apology (this commitment had evaporated by the 2004 election but Labor's result did not improve). Commentators have stressed the obvious role played by the issue of asylum seekers in determining voting patterns, yet the insistence on racial overtones as displayed by the Liberal leadership should indicate that indigenous reconciliation and refugees are overlapping concerns. For an analysis of the re-emergence of racial discourse in 1990s Australia, see A. Markus, *Race: John Howard and the Remaking of Australia*, Sydney: Allen & Unwin, 2001. On the necessity of enacting a treaty between indigenous Australia and the wider polity, see S. Brennan, L. Behrendt, L. Strelein and G. Williams, *Treaty*, Sydney: Federation Press, 2005.

56. D. Denoon, 'The Isolation of Australian History', *Historical Studies*, 87, 1986, pp. 252–60.

57. Attwood, 'Mabo, Australia and the end of History', p. 116.

58. One should mention here that in both countries it was the judiciary that played an essential part in bringing about the more visible institutional transformations. Of course, the conservative opinion

has always argued against the interventionism of the judiciary power.

59. On Aboriginal sovereignty, see L. Behrendt, *Achieving Social Justice: Indigenous Rights and Australia's Future*, Sydney: Federation Press, 2003.

60. P. Read, *Belonging: Australians, Place and Aboriginal Ownership*, Melbourne: Cambridge University Press, 2000.

Chapter 5 Conclusion: Imperial Engagements and the Negotiation of Israel and Palestine

1. A. Curthoys, *Freedom Ride: A Freedom Rider Remembers*, Sydney: Allen & Unwin, 2002.

2. For a compelling analysis of the politics of representation of the Israeli–Palestinian confrontation, see G. Philo and M. Berry, *Bad News From Israel*, London: Pluto Press, 2004. For insightful analyses of the dynamics of perception in the US, see K. Christison, *Perceptions of Palestine: Their Influence on U.S. Middle East Policy*, Berkeley: University of California Press, 1999; and N. H. Aruri, *Dishonest Broker: The US Role in Israel and Palestine*, Cambridge, MA: South End Press, 2003.

3. For an analysis of a long history of US cultural production associated with the Middle East, see D. Little, *American Orientalism: The United States and the Middle East since 1945*, London and New York: I. B. Tauris, 2002.

4. For example, see E. W. Said, 'America's Last Taboo', *New Left Review*, 6. Said, however, concentrates on the role of the Zionist lobby in American public life.

5. See A. Cockburn and J. St. Clair (eds), *The politics of anti-Semitism*, Petrolia, CA: CounterPunch, 2003; and S. Halimi, 'Aux Etats-Unis, M. Ariel Sharon n'a que des amis', *Le Monde Diplomatique*, July 2003, pp. 12–13.

6. However, this overlap is not a recent phenomenon and the notion that the US is 'God's American Israel' is grounded in a very long tradition of US political thought. As noted by Douglas Little, the 'revolutionary statesmen who invented America in the quarter-century after 1776 regarded the Muslim world, beset by oriental despotism, economic squalor, and intellectual stultification, as the antithesis of the republicanism to which they had pledged their sacred honor', Little, *American Orientalism*, p. 12.

7. While one important trend in this context has been a long-lasting process of incorporating a specific version of Holocaust memory in American public imagination – an example of a victimological narrative authorizing violence – the American Jewish Committee

has recently published a study where a structural similarity between anti-Semitism and anti-Americanism was noted and highlighted. See, for example, A. Mintz, *Popular Culture and the Shaping of Holocaust Memory in America*, Seattle: University of Washington Press, 2001; and A. Rosenfeld, *Anti-Americanism and Anti-Semitism: A New Front of Zealotry*, New York: American Jewish Committee, 2003.

8. See N. Guttman, 'Top U.S. advisers to address AIPAC meet', *Haaretz*, 14/10/04.

9. See N. Guttman, 'U.S. Congress backs anti-Semitism law', *Haaretz*, 14/10/04.

10. Last time he was seen with a book, he was reading *My Pet Goat* to primary-school children on September 11, 2001. See C. Murphy, 'Bush's New Book for a New Term', *BBC News*, 21/01/05. The URL for this article is <http://news.bbc.co.uk/2/hi/americas/4195303.stm>.

11. In fact, the background to this remarkable publicity incident is very complicated and includes Tom Bernstein, a businessman involved in George W. Bush's ascendancy. *Haaretz* journalist Amir Oren has described an intense network of two-way connections: 'If Bush owes anything to Bernstein, who wants to help Sharansky, that was enough, but just to be sure, a second mortgage was taken out in the name of the person who wrote the book "with" Sharansky, Ron Dermer, who is also close to Finance Minister Benjamin Netanyahu and whose brother David Dermer is mayor of Miami Beach, which was once also headed by their father. Ron Dermer worked for a Republican strategist, and David is a Democrat, but Florida Governor Jeb Bush helped him get elected, and Dermer helped out Jeb's brother and endorsed him instead of John Kerry (who, said Dermer, called Arafat a statesman, and was against the security fence) during the race for every vote in Florida. The Dermer family helped the Bush family; the Bush family helps the Dermer family. After Bush won, in Florida and America, Sharansky and his helper Dermer were invited to the meeting with Rice – she doesn't deny that she has to read what her boss reads, both to be ready for his questions and to prepare him an executive brief – and from there to the president. The target was captured, the recommendation was disseminated: It was Bush's mouth, Sharansky's voice. Seemingly, that's where the plot should end, but it continues. Ron Dermer, who lives in Jerusalem, has just been named the economic attache in the Israeli Embassy in Washington and goes to work there in another month. A personal acquaintance with Bush and Rice and influential people like Newt Gingrich, the former speaker of the house, is going to be very helpful when it comes to meeting other

people in the uppermost levels of the administration', A. Oren, 'Bro, talk to his brother', *Haaretz*, 01/02/05. Natan Sharansky quit the government in early May 2005.

12. For an insight into the day-to-day functioning of the special relationship between Sharon's and Bush's offices – a relationship that strategically blurs the distinction between Israeli and US administrations, see Dov Weisglass's interview with *Haaretz*, released in October 2004: 'The channel between [Condoleezza] Rice and me [Dov Weisglass] has two main purposes. One is to advance processes that are initiated, to examine our ideas and their ideas. The road map, for example, or the disengagement plan. But there is an equally important function, which is troubleshooting. If something happens – an unusual military operation, a hitch, a targeted assassination that succeeded or one that didn't succeed – before it becomes an imbroglio, she calls me and says, "We saw so-and-so on CNN. What's going on?" And I say, "Condy, the usual 10 minutes?" She laughs and we hang up. Ten minutes later, after I find out what happened, I get back to her and tell her the whole truth. The whole truth. I tell her and she takes it down: this is what we intended, this is how it came out. She doesn't get worked up. She believes us. The continuation is damage control', A. Shavit, 'The big freeze', *Haaretz*, 08/10/04.

13. See E. Salpeter, 'The Jewish World/Such a thing as too much support for Israel', *Haaretz*, 05/10/04. In April 2005 AIPAC dismissed two senior officials involved in the matter and abandoned previous protestations that nothing illegal had been done.

14. See, for example, Nathan Guttman, 'The messiah wars', *Haaretz*, 14/10/04. In his analysis of Evangelical missionary activities among American Jews, Guttman refers for example to one 'Presbyterian Church, which runs Avodat Yisrael – a sort of church-cum-synagogue in the Philadelphia area [and] makes use of Jewish symbols and invites Jews to participate in ceremonies and services with the aim of bringing them into the ranks of Christianity'. Of course, the success of these activities should not be measured in their capacity to actually convert many of the individuals they target; however, these endeavours contribute significantly to the increasing identification of US Evangelical constituencies with Israel.

15. See J. Yovel, 'Security or insecurity?', *Haaretz*, 12/11/04 (reviewing *In the Name of Security*, special issue of *Adalah's Review*, 4, 2004).

16. For an example of this trend, see Alan Morton Dershowitz, *Why Terrorism Works: Understanding the Threat, Responding to the Challenge*, New Haven, CT: Yale University Press, 2002. Among other considerations, Dershowitz interprets recent terrorist activity

against the United States as a result of the Oslo peace process, where a 'terrorist' organization was acknowledged as a legitimate partner for negotiations. Following this logic, he could as well consider September 11 as one consequence of the British government decision to negotiate with a 'terrorist' organization at the end of the American War of Independence.

17. Quoted in Little, *American Orientalism*, p. 24.

18. On the architecture of the occupation, see D. Monk, *An Aesthetic Occupation: The Immediacy of Architecture and the Palestine Conflict*, Durham, NC: Duke University Press, 2001; and E. Zandberg, 'Surroundings/Watch this space', *Haaretz*, 14/10/04 (which reviews 'Territories, Live', an exhibition dealing with the politics of architecture in the Occupied Territories). After appearing in galleries in the US and Europe, 'Territories, Live' was also staged in Israel.

19. During the summer vacation of 2003, more than a hundred members of the US Congress and the mayor of New York visited Israel, expressing solidarity. While this is a traditional period for US representatives to get in touch with their constituencies, it can be assumed that in the specific conditions of the current political climate, travelling to Israel is one very effective way to respond to the concerns of an anxious electorate. See J. Lis, 'New York Mayor Bloomberg Visits Bombing Site, Victims', *Haaretz*, 29/08/03.

20. See Ella Shoat, 'Antinomies of Exile: Said at the Frontier of National Narrations', in M. Sprinker (ed.), *Edward Said: A Critical Reader*, Oxford: Blackwell, 1992, pp. 121–43. Shoat writes about the affinities in settler and religious consciousness between Israel and the United States.

21. Quoted in J. Weisberg, *More George W. Bushisms*, New York: Freeside, 2002, p. 84.

22. This wouldn't be the first time. Imperial imagination and colonial circumstances in the area have a long history of mutual entanglement. See J. Hamilton, 'How the Old Testament Went Full Circle – From Jerusalem to England and Back to Jerusalem', in J. Hamilton, *God, Guns and Israel: Britain, the First World War and the Jews in the Holy City*, Stroud: Sutton, 2004, pp. 17–101.

23. See, for example, L. Veracini, 'Colonialism and Genocides: Towards an Analysis of the Settler Archive of the European Imagination', in D. Moses (ed.), *Genocide and Colonialism*, New York: Berghahn Books (forthcoming).

24. After all, what is more indicative of a colonial state of mind than then neo-neocandidate for the Labor Party leadership Ehud Barak's May 2005 passing remark about the necessity of Israel proposing the international community 'to give itself a mandate over the

Palestinian territories to assist the Palestinian Authority in preparing for the establishment of a Palestinian state'? See A. Shavit, 'Secrets and Lies', *Haaretz*, 19/05/05. A call for an understanding of the colonially determined character of Israeli public discourse was recently presented in *Haaretz* by professor of political geography at Ben Gurion University Oren Yiftachel in 'Ending the colonialism', *Haaretz*, 19/07/05.

25. For example, see J. Halper, 'Beyond Road Maps and Walls', *The Link*, 1, 2004. The URL for this article is <http:/www.one-state.org/articles/2004/halper.htm>. Halper's analysis covers the confinement of Palestinians to Areas A and B, systematic closures; settlement blocs (as opposed to isolated settlements), permanent infrastructure, and the US $2 billion separation barrier.

26. M. Tarazi, 'Why not two peoples, one state', *New York Times*, 04/10/04.

27. See A. Tal, 'The PLO still sees a single state', *Haaretz*, 14/10/04, and B. Rubin, 'One more Palestinian mistake', *Jerusalem Post*, 12/10/04.

28. Rubin, 'One More Palestinian mistake'.

29. See M. Benvenisti, 'The injustice of the new formula', *Haaretz*, 22/10/04.

30. Z. Sternhell, 'Wanted: a mental revolution', *Haaretz*, 01/07/05.

31. Quite interestingly, ultra-Orthodox Member of Parliament Avraham Ravitz has published a 'peace' plan according to which settlers will not be evacuated and will remain in their settlements holding dual Israeli and Palestinian citizenship (Ravitz explains that there is no *mitzvah* [commandment] to rule the land, only to settle in it). While this proposal may be relevant to a number of religious settlers, the majority of settlers would find it impossible to live in a Palestinian-dominated body politic. Perplexed Israeli reactions to this plan indicate that when it comes to the settlement enterprise, colonialism beats religion: after all, Fanon had noted that 'the settler, from the moment the colonial context disappears, has no longer an interest in remaining or in co-existing'. See S. Ilan, 'The Ravitz initiative', *Haaretz*, 20/01/05; and F. Fanon, *The Wretched of the Earth*, London: Penguin, 1967, p. 35.

32. A fourth model of postcolonial movement, entailing a diasporic separation between citizenship and statehood for Palestinian refugees, would also be needed. On this issue, see, for example, the director of the Palestinian Diaspora and Refugee Center in Ramallah, Sari Hanafi's analysis, 'The Broken Boundaries of Statehood and Citizenship', *Bitterlemons*, 15/03/04. The URL containing this article is <http://www.bitterlemons.org/previous/bl150304ed10.html#is2>.

33. Significantly, Yonatan Bassi – the man in charge of the practicalities of
     the disengagement process, heading the administrative body charged
     with the resettlement of evacuated settlers – does not envisage
     complete separation between Israelis and the Palestinians of the
     Occupied Territories: 'The large context of the disengagement plan
     is two states for two peoples. That is clear. Only the establishment
     of a Palestinian state will save the Jewish state. But it is clear to
     me today that it will be impossible to continue along the path in
     which there is an Arab minority in the Jewish state, but no Jewish
     minority in the Palestinian state ... Therefore I think that Israel
     should allow those Jews who so desire, to remain as a minority in
     Palestinian territory in the future. It will be far better if there are 20
     per cent Arabs on this side of the line and 20 per cent Jews on the
     other side of the line. Anyone who forgoes that demand is forgoing
     the demand for peace ... If the need arises to evacuate, it will be
     done. If lines have to be shortened, lines will be shortened. But as a
     comprehensive solution, evacuation is not the right solution. It is not
     a solution of peace. The right solution is two states for two people
     with two large minorities', A. Shavit, 'Dividing the Land/Balancing
     act', *Haaretz*, 08/07/05.

34. Former US Secretary of State Henry Kissinger published an article
     in late 2004 where he criticized the abandonment of a long-lasting
     diplomatic/political drive aiming at separating two bodies politic
     and suggested implementing drastic measures to bring about a viable
     two-state solution characterized by reciprocal ethnic exclusion:
     'The territorial dividing line should be defined by a security fence
     paralleling the 1967 borders along principles discussed at Camp
     David and Taba. This would return all the West Bank to Palestinian
     rule except some 5 to 8 per cent needed for the strategic defense of
     Israel. In return, Israel would transfer some of its current territory
     to the Palestinian state. Israel has made the offer of compensation
     at Camp David but has identified parts of the Negev – the southern
     desert – for that purpose. It would be wiser to transfer territory with
     significant Arab populations from the northern part of Israel. Such
     a transfer would be symbolically more significant, but would also
     ease the demographic problem. Israeli settlements located beyond
     the dividing line would be subject to Palestinian jurisdiction, which
     would probably imply their abandonment.' This piece was published
     in a number of daily newspapers, see, for example, H. Kissinger,
     'Opportunities for resolving conflict in the Middle East', *San Diego
     Union Tribune*, 05/12/04.

Bibliography

Adam, H., Adam, K. and Moodley, K. 2004, 'Conditions for Peacemaking: Negotiating the Non-negotiable in South Africa and the Middle East', in Schneckener, U. and Wolff, S. (eds), *Managing and Settling Ethnic Conflicts*, London: Hurst & Company.

Agamben, G. 1995, *Homo Sacer*, Torino: Einaudi.

Alexander, M. S., Evans, M. and Keiger, J. F. V. (eds) 2002, *The Algerian War and the French Army, 1954–62: Experiences, Images, Testimonies*, London: Palgrave Macmillan.

Alpher, Y. 2003, 'Hard Questions, Tough Answers: A weekly APN Q & A with Yossi Alpher June 2, 2003', Americans for Peace Now, 02/06/03 <http://www.peacenow.org/nia/briefs/QA060203.html>.

Anderson, B. 1991, *Imagined Communities: Reflections on the Origin and Spread of Nationalism*, London and New York: Verso.

Anderson, B. 1998, *The Spectre of Comparisons: Nationalism, Southeast Asia, and the World*, New York: Verso.

Anderson, P. 2001, 'Scurrying towards Bethlehem', *New Left Review*, 10.

Arad, G. N. (ed.) 1995, *Israeli Historiography Revisited*, special edition of *History and Memory*, 7, 1.

Arens, M. 2004, 'They fought for the country', *Haaretz*, 21/12/04.

Aron, R. 1958, *L'Algérie et la République*, Paris: Plon.

Aruri N. H. (ed.) 2001, *Palestinian Refugees: The Right of Return*, London: Pluto Press.

Aruri, N. H. 2003, *Dishonest Broker: The US Role in Israel and Palestine*, Cambridge, MA: South End Press.

Ash, G. 2004, 'Diagnosing Benny Morris; the mind of a European settler', *YellowTimes.org*, 24/01/04 <http://www.yellowtimes.org/article.php?sid=1750>.

Attwood, B. 1996, 'Mabo, Australia and the end of History', in Attwood, B. (ed.), *In the Age of Mabo: History, Aborigines and Australia*, Sydney: Allen and Unwin.

Attwood, B. 2001, 'A Tour of Duty in Australia's History Wars', *Australian Financial Review*, 01/06/2001.

Attwood, B. 2005, *Telling the Truth about Aboriginal History*, Sydney: Allen & Unwin.

Attwood, B. and Foster, S. G. (eds) 2003, *Frontier Conflict: The Australian Experience*, Canberra: National Museum of Australia.

Aussaresses, P. 2002, *The Battle of the Casbah: Terrorism and Counter-terrorism in Algeria, 1955–1957*, New York: Enigma Books.

Australian Women's Weekly 2001, 'Interview with Helen Clark', *The Australian Women's Weekly*, November issue.

Balibar, E. 2004, 'Universalité de la cause palestinienne', *Le Monde Diplomatique*, May issue.

Barnett, M. N. (ed.) 1996, *Israel in Comparative Perspective: Challenging the Conventional Wisdom*, Albany, NY: SUNY Press.

Barzilai, G. 2003, *Politics and Cultures of Legal Identities: Communities and Law*, Ann Arbor: University of Michigan Press.

BBC News, 'Hamas displays "Israeli remains"', *BBC News*, 05/12/04.

Behrendt, L. 2003, *Achieving Social Justice: Indigenous Rights and Australia's Future*, Sydney: Federation Press.

Benn, A. 2004, 'Israel talks with UN, US on post-pullout status of territories', *Haaretz*, 22/11/04.

Benn, A. 2004, 'PM summons chief of staff to clarify his criticism of pullout', *Haaretz*, 09/03/04.

Benn, A. 2004, 'Tactical victory, strategic debacle', *Haaretz*, 14/07/04.

Benn, A. and Verter, Y. 2005, 'Even King Solomon ceded territories', *Haaretz*, 22/04/05.

Ben Simhon, K. 2004, 'The outsider', *Haaretz*, 17/09/04.

Benvenisti, M. 1999, 'The Illusion of Soft Borders', *Haaretz*, 14/10/99.

Benvenisti, M. 2004, 'Democracy, but not here', *Haaretz*, 02/12/04.

Benvenisti, M. 2004, 'The injustice of the new formula', *Haaretz*, 22/10/04.

Benvenisti, M. 2004, 'What lies at the bottom of the barrel', *Haaretz*, 12/08/04.

Benvenisti, M. 2005, 'Apartheid misses the point', *Haaretz*, 19/05/05.

Benziman, U. 2004, 'Victors beware', *Haaretz*, 26/09/04.

Benziman, U. 2005, 'So sorry we didn't win', *Haaretz*, 08/05/05.

Betts, R. B. 1961, *Assimilation and Association in French Colonial Theory, 1890–1914*, New York: Columbia University Press.

Bird, C. (ed.) 1998, *The Stolen Children: Their Stories*, Sydney: Random House.

Bishara, M. 2001, *Israel/Palestine: Peace or Apartheid*, London: Zed Books.

Bornstein, A. S. 2002, *Crossing the Green Line between the West Bank and Israel*, Philadelphia: University of Pennsylvania Press.

Branche, R. 2001, *La Torture et l'armée pendant la guerre d'Algérie*, Paris: Gallimard.

Brawley, S. 1996, 'A Comfortable and Relaxed Past: John Howard and the 'Battle of History' – The First Phase, February 1992 to March 1996', *The Electronic Journal of Australian and New Zealand History*, 1 <http://www.jcu.edu.au/aff/history/articles/brawley.htm>.

Brennan, S., Behrendt, L., Strelein, L. and Williams, G. 2005, *Treaty*, Sydney: Federation Press.

Broome, R. 1994, 'Aboriginal Victims and Voyagers, Confronting Frontier Myths', *Journal of Australian Studies*, 42.

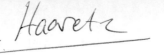

Brubaker, R. 1996, 'Aftermaths of Empire and the Unmixing of Peoples', in Brubaker, R., *Nationalism Reframed: Nationhood and the National Question in the New Europe*, Cambridge: Cambridge University Press.

Brunton, R. 1998, 'Genocide, the "Stolen Generations", and the "Unconceived Generations"', *Quadrant*, May issue.

Burston, B. 2004, 'Background/Sharon's do-or-die Gaza plan – or is it do AND die?' *Haaretz*, 11/03/04.

Burston, B. 2004, 'Background: The war that Palestine couldn't lose – and did', *Haaretz*, 01/10/04.

Burston, B. 2005, 'Background/The 3rd Intifada: Settlers take on their own Army', *Haaretz*, 06/01/05.

Buruma, I. 2002, 'Do not treat Israel like Apartheid South Africa', *Guardian*, 23/07/02.

Caplan, N. 1995, 'The "New Historians"', *Journal of Palestine Studies*, XXIV, 4.

Carey, R. (ed.) 2001, *The New Intifada: Resisting Israel's Apartheid*, New York: Verso.

Carey, R. and Shanin, J. 2002, *The Other Israel: Voices of Refusal and Dissent*, New York: New Press.

Chafer, T. 2002, *The End of Empire in French West Africa: France's Successful Decolonization?*, Oxford: Berg.

Chesterman, J. and Galligan, B. 1997, *Citizens Without Rights: Aborigines and Australian Citizenship*, Melbourne: Cambridge University Press.

Choo, C. and Hollbach, S. (eds) 2003, *History and Native Title*, Perth: University of Western Australia Press.

Christison, K. 1999, *Perceptions of Palestine: Their Influence on U.S. Middle East Policy*, Berkeley: University of California Press.

Christison, K. 2001, *The Wound of Dispossession: Telling the Palestinian Story*, Santa Fe, NM: Sunlit Hills Press.

Clayton, A. 1994, *The French Wars of Decolonization*, London: Longman.

Cleary, J. 2002, *Literature, Partition and the Nation-State: Culture and Conflict in Ireland, Israel and Palestine*, Cambridge and New York: Cambridge University Press.

Cockburn, A. and St. Clair, J. (eds) 2003, *The politics of anti-Semitism*, Petrolia, CA: CounterPunch.

Cogan, C. G. 2002, 'France, the United States and the Invisible Algerian Outcome', *Journal of Strategic Studies*, 25, 2.

Cohen, S. P., Hudson, M. C., Guttman, N. and Jahshan, K. E. 2003, 'Is a Two-State Solution Still Viable?', *Middle East Policy*, 2.

Coker, C. 1986, *The United States and South Africa, 1968–1985: Constructive Engagement and its Critics*, Durham, NC: Duke University Press.

Conklin, A. L. 1998, *A Mission to Civilize: The Republican Idea of Empire in France and West Africa, 1895–1930*, Stanford, CA: Stanford University Press.

Crais, C. 1992, *White Supremacy amd Black Resistance in Pre-Industrial South Africa: the Making of the Colonial Order in the Eastern Cape, 1770–1865*, Cambridge: Cambridge University Press.

Cramer, R. B. 2004, *How Israel Lost: The Four Questions*, New York: Simon & Schuster.

Curthoys, A. and Docker, J. (eds) 2001, *'Genocide'? Australian Aboriginal History in International Perspective*, special issue of *Aboriginal History*, 25.

Curthoys, A. 2002, *Freedom Ride: A Freedom Rider Remembers*, Sydney: Allen & Unwin.

Davis, U. 1987, *Israel: An Apartheid State*, London: Zed Books.

Davis, U. 2003, *Apartheid Israel: Possibilities for the Struggle Within*, London: Zed Books.

Day, D. 2001, *Claiming a Continent: A New History of Australia*, Sydney: HarperCollins.

Dayan, A. 2005, 'How did Jewish settlements begin? It's a secret', *Haaretz*, 29/03/05.

Denoon, D. 1986, 'The Isolation of Australian History', *Historical Studies*, 87.

Dershowitz, A. M. 2002, *Why Terrorism Works: Understanding the Threat, Responding to the Challenge*, New Haven, CT: Yale University Press.

Drew, A. 2000, *Discordant Comrades: Identities and Loyalties on the South African Left*, Aldershot: Ashgate.

Dromi, U. 2002, 'Illuminating the dark alleys of decolonization', *Haaretz*, 17/07/02.

Economist 2004, 'Israeli and Palestinians: Voices from the Frontline', *The Economist*, 21/02/04.

Eisen, H. 2005, 'At U of T, Arab students' event draws controversy', *Globe and Mail*, 31/01/05.

Eldar, A. 2003, 'People and Politics/Sharon's Bantustans are far from Copenhagen's hope', *Haaretz*, 14/05/03.

Eldar, A. 2004, 'Learning all the wrong facts', *Haaretz*, 09/12/04.

Elkins, C. and Pedersen, S. (eds) 2005, *Settler Colonialism in the Twentieth Century: Projects, Practices, Legacies*, London and New York: Routledge.

Elmer, J. 2003, 'Israel and the Empire: Jeff Halper interview', *FromOccupiedpalestine.org*, 20/09/03 <http://www.fromoccupied palestine.org/index.php?or=64>.

Ettinger, Y. 2004, 'Druze torn in their relationship with state', *Haaretz*, 19/12/04.

Evans, R. and Thorpe, B. 2001, 'Indigenocide and the Massacre of Aboriginal History', *Overland*, 163.

Fanon, F. 1967, *The Wretched of the Earth*, London: Penguin Books.

Fanon, F. 1970, *Black Skin White Masks*, St. Albans: Paladin.

Farsakh, L. 2003, 'Israel: An Apartheid State?' *Le Monde Diplomatique*, English edition, November issue <http://mondediplo.com/2003/11/04apartheid>.

Fels, M. 1988, *Good Men and True: The Aboriginal Police of the Port Phillip District, 1837–1853*, Melbourne: Melbourne University Press.

Fieldhouse, D. K. 1981, *Colonialism, 1870–1945: An Introduction*, New York: St. Martin's Press.

Finkelstein, N. G. 1995, *Image and Reality of the Israel-Palestine Conflict*, London and New York: Verso.

Fischbach, M. R. 2003, *Records of Dispossession: Palestinian Refugee Property and the Arab-Israeli Conflict*, New York: Columbia University Press.

Fisk, R. 2002, 'In on the tide, the guns and rockets that fuel this fight', *Independent*, 29/04/02.

Foundation for Middle East Peace 2003, 'Pilots' Letter', October <http://www.fmep.org/analysis/PilotsLetter10-2003.html>.

Fox, E. 2002, *Palestine Twilight: Murder and Malice in the Holy Land*, Sydney: HarperCollins Australia.

Frémeaux, J. 2002, *La France et l'Algérie en guerre: 1830–1870, 1954–1962*, Paris: Commission Française d'Histoire Militaire/Institut de stratégie comparée.

Galili, L. 2004, 'The devil's own disengagement', *Haaretz*, 06/10/04.

Galili, L. 2004, 'Lieberman: Transfer Arab areas of Jerusalem to Palestinians', *Haaretz*, 17/12/04.

Gidron, B., Katz, S. N. and Hasenfeld, Y. 2002, *Conflict Resolution in Northern Ireland, South Africa, and Israel/Palestine*, Oxford: Oxford University Press.

Godimer, N. 2003, 'New Introduction', in Memmi, A., *The Colonizer and the Colonized*, London: Earthscan.

Goodall, H. 1996, *Invasion to Embassy: Land in Aboriginal Politics in New South Wales, 1770–1972*, Sydney: Allen & Unwin.

Grattan, M. (ed.) 2000, *Essays in Australian Reconciliation*, Melbourne: Bookman Press.

Gregory, D. 2004, *The Colonial Present: Afghanistan, Palestine, Iraq*, Malden: Blackwell Publishers.

Gresh, A. 2003, *Israël-Palestine. Vérités sur un conflit*, Paris: Hachette.

Guttman, N. 2004, 'The messiah wars', *Haaretz*, 14/10/04.

Guttman, N. 2004, 'Top U.S. advisers to address AIPAC meet', *Haaretz*, 14/10/04.

Guttman, N. 2004, 'U.S. Congress backs anti-Semitism law', *Haaretz*, 14/10/04.

Guttman, N. 2004, 'A warning signal from the churches', *Haaretz*, 26/11/04.

Guyatt, N. 1998, *The Absence of Peace: Understanding the Israel–Palestinian Conflict*, London: Zed Books.

Haaretz 2004, 'The brass must be quiet', *Haaretz*, 26/09/04.

Haaretz 2004, 'The dangers of the rabbis' declaration', *Haaretz*, 09/09/04.

Haaretz 2004, 'The Disengagement Plan of Prime Minister Ariel Sharon', *Haaretz*, 01/04/04.

Haaretz 2004, 'Foreign Ministry warns Israel, Europe on collision course', *Haaretz*, 13/10/04.

Haaretz 2004, 'It can happen here', *Haaretz*, 22/11/04.

Haaretz 2004, 'The routine of death', *Haaretz*, 09/03/04.

Haaretz 2005, 'Racist legislation', *Haaretz*, 18/01/05.

Haaretz 2005, 'Toward the edge of the abyss', *Haaretz*, 19/07/05.

Haaretz 2005, 'When everything is possible', *Haaretz*, 06/06/05.

Haebich, A. 2000, *Broken Circles: Fragmenting Indigenous Families, 1800–2000*, Fremantle: Fremantle Arts Centre Press.

Haebich, A. 2005, 'The Battlefields of Aboriginal History', in Lyons, M. and Russell, P. (eds), *Australia's History: Themes and Debates*, Sydney: University of New South Wales Press.

Hage, G. 2003, *Against Paranoid Nationalism: Searching for Hope in a Shrinking Society*, Sydney: Pluto Press.

Hajjar, L. 2005, *Courting Conflict: The Israeli Military Court System in the West Bank and Gaza*, Berkeley: University of California Press.

Halimi, S. 2003, 'Aux Etats-Unis, M. Ariel Sharon n'a que des amis', *Le Monde Diplomatique*, July issue.

Halper, J. 2000, 'The 94 Percent Solution: A Matrix of Control', *Middle East Report*, 216.

Halper, J. 2001, 'The Three Jerusalems', ICAHD, 06/01/01.

Halper, J. 2002, '*Nishul* (Displacement): Israel's form of Apartheid', Institute of African Studies, School of International and Public Affairs, Columbia University, 20/09/02 <http://www.columbia.edu/cu/sipa/REGIONAL/IAS/documents/apartheid.doc>.

Halper, J. 2003, 'Post-apartheid: One State', UN International Conference on Civil Society in Support of the Palestinian People, New York, 05/09/03 <http://fromoccupiedpalestine.org/node.php?id=772>.

Halper, J. 2004, 'Beyond Road Maps and Walls', *The Link*, 1 <http:/www.one-state.org/articles/2004/halper.htm>.

Halper, J. no date, 'The Key to Peace: Dismantling the Matrix of Control', ICAHD <http://www.icahd.org/eng/articles>.

Hamilton, J. 2004, 'How the Old Testament Went Full Circle – From Jerusalem to England and Back to Jerusalem', in J. Hamilton, *God, Guns and Israel: Britain, the First World War and the Jews in the Holy City*, Stroud: Sutton.

Hanafi, S. 2004, 'The Broken Boundaries of Statehood and Citizenship', *Bitterlemons*, 15/03/04 <http://www.bitterlemons.org/previous/bl150304ed10.html#is2>.

Harel, A. 2004, 'Analysis/Not the Last Attempt', *Haaretz*, 07/03/04.

Harel, A. 2004, 'Analysis/Reminders of Lebanon', *Haaretz*, 12/05/04.

Harel, A. 2004, 'One Friday afternoon four years ago', *Haaretz*, 12/09/04.

Harel, A. 2005, 'Palestinian corpse used for IDF anatomy lesson', *Haaretz*, 28/01/05.

Harel, A. 2005, 'Dozens of psychologists to help IDF soldiers to cope with Gaza pullout', *Haaretz*, 28/06/05.

Harel, A. and Yoaz, Y. 2005, 'IDF soldier convicted of manslaughter of British activist', *Haaretz*, 28/06/05.

Haroun, A. 1986, *La 7e Wilaya: La Guerre de FLN en France, 1854–1962*, Paris: Seuil.

Hass, A. 2003, 'The Wall: Palestinians Now "Illegal Residents"; IDF redefines Palestinians West of the Fence', *Haaretz*, 14/10/03.

Hass, A. 2004, 'Qalandiyah in the rain', *Haaretz*, 24/11/04.

Hasson, N. 2005, 'Extremists resorting to scare tactics against disengagement', *Haaretz*, 17/01/05.

Horne, A. 2002, *A Savage War of Peace: Algeria 1954–1962*, London: Pan, 2002.

Human Rights and Equal Opportunity Commission 1996, *Bringing Them Home, Report of the National Inquiry Into the Separation of Aboriginal and Torres Strait Islander Children from their Families*, Canberra: Commonwealth Printer.

Ilan, S. 2005, 'The Ravitz initiative', *Haaretz*, 20/01/05.

Inbar, E. 2004, 'The End of the Palestinian Option', *Haaretz*, 23/03/04.

Jabarin, H. 2005, 'From discrimination to the denial of basic freedoms', *Haaretz*, 18/05/05.

Judt, T. 2002, 'Israel's Road to Nowhere', *New York Review of Books*, 09/05/02.

Kapeliouk, A. 2002, 'Retour sur les raisons de l'échec de Camp David', *Le Monde Diplomatique*, February issue.

Karsh, E. 1997, *Fabricating Israeli History: The 'New Historians'*, London: Frank Cass.

Keegan, T. 1996, *Colonial South Africa and the Origins of the Racial Order*, London: Leicester University Press.

Keinon, H. 2003, 'Some Precedents', *Jerusalem Post*, 08/05/03.

Khalidi, R. 1997, *Palestinian Identity: The Construction of Modern National Consciousness*, New York: Columbia University Press.

Kimmerling, B. 1983, *Zionism and Territory*, Berkeley: University of California Press.

Kimmerling, B. 2001, *The Invention and Decline of Israeliness: State, Society, and the Military*, Berkeley: University of California Press.

Kimmerling, B. 2002, 'Jurisdiction in an Immigrant-Settler Society: The "Jewish and Democratic State"', *Comparative Political Studies*, 35, 10.

Kimmerling, B. 2003, 'From Barak to the Road Map', *New Left Review*, 23.

Kimmerling, B. 2003, *Politicide: Ariel Sharon's War Against the Palestinians*, New York: Verso.

Kimmerling, B. 2004, 'Benny Morris's Shocking Interview', *History News Network*, 26/01/04.

Kimmerling, B. and Migda, J. S. 2003, *The Palestinian People: A History*, Cambridge, MA: Harvard University Press.

Kissinger, H. 2004, 'Opportunities for resolving conflict in the Middle East', *San Diego Union Tribune*, 05/12/04.

Krauthammer, C. 2004, 'Israel's Intifada Victory', *Washington Post*, 18/06/04.

Laor, Y. 2002, 'Diary', *London Review of Books*, 03/10/02 <http://www.lrb.co.uk/v24/n19/laor01_.html>.

Laor, Y. 2004, 'Al-mahsum, mahsom, checkpoint', *Haaretz*, 02/12/04.

Laor, Y. 2005, 'Referendum means apartheid', *Haaretz*, 03/02/05.

Laqueur, W. 1972, *A History of Zionism*, London: Weidenfeld and Nicolson.

Lester, A. 1996, *From Colonization to Democracy: A New Historical Geography of South Africa*, London: Tauris Academic Studies.

Levy, D. 2005, 'Coordination is not negotiation', *Haaretz*, 21/01/05.

Levy, G. 2005, 'The growing gap between the protected and the unprotected', *Haaretz*, 12/06/05.

Levy, G. 2005, 'No border between Yesha and the IDF', *Haaretz*, 06/02/05.

Lis, J. 2003, 'New York Mayor Bloomberg Visits Bombing Site, Victims', *Haaretz*, 29/08/03.

Little, D. 2002, *American Orientalism: The United States and the Middle East since 1945*, London and New York: I. B. Tauris.

Loos, N. 1996, *Edward Koiki Mabo: His Life and Struggle for Land Rights*, Brisbane: University of Queensland Press.

Low, D. A. 1991, 'The Contraction of England: An Inaugural Lecture, 1984', in D. A. Low, *Eclipse of Empire*, Cambridge: Cambridge University Press.

Lustik, I. S. 1993, *Unsettled States, Disputed Lands: Britain & Ireland, France & Algeria, Israel & the West Bank/Gaza*, Ithaca, NY: Cornell University Press.

Lyman, P. N. 2002, *Partner to History: the U.S. Role in South Africa's Transition to Democracy*, Washington, DC: United States Institute of Peace Press.

Macintyre, S. and Clark, A. 2003, *The History Wars*, Melbourne: Melbourne University Press.

Malley, R. and Agha, H. 2001, 'Camp David: The Tragedy of Errors', *New York Review of Books*, 09/08/01.

Malley, R. and Agha, H. 2005, 'The Last Palestinian', *New York Review of Books*, 10/02/05.

Manne, R. 2001, *In Denial: the Stolen Generation and the Right*, Melbourne: Black Inc.

Manne, R. (ed.) 2003, *Whitewash: On Keith Windschuttle's Fabrication of Aboriginal History*, Melbourne: Black Inc.

Mannoni, O. 1964, *Prospero and Caliban: The Psychology of Colonization*, New York: Praeger.

Marcus, Y. 2004, 'Get down from the roof you crazies', *Haaretz*, 05/10/04.

Marcus, Y. 2004, 'Six comments on the situation', *Haaretz*, 01/10/04.

Marcus, Y. 2005, 'Get down from the rooftops', *Haaretz*, 19/07/05.

Markus, A. 2001, *Race: John Howard and the Remaking of Australia*, Sydney: Allen & Unwin.

Masalha, N. 1991, *Expulsion of the Palestinians: the Concept of 'Transfer' in Zionist Political Thought, 1882–1984*, Washington, DC: Institute of Palestine Studies.

Masalha, N. 2000, *Imperial Israel and the Palestinians*, London: Pluto Press.

Mathieu, A. 2004, 'Jean-Paul Sartre et la guerre d'Algérie', *Le Monde Diplomatique*, November issue.

May, D. 1994, *Aboriginal Labour and the Cattle Industry: Queensland from White Settlement to Present*, Melbourne: Cambridge University Press.

McGeal, C. 2003, 'We're air force pilots, not mafia. We don't take revenge', *Guardian*, 03/12/03.

McGeal, C. 2004, 'Anglican group calls for Israel sanctions: Campaigners inspired by boycott of apartheid South Africa', *Guardian*, 24/09/04.

McGrath, A. 1987, *'Born in the Cattle': Aborigines in Cattle Country*, Sydney: Allen & Unwin.

Memmi, A. 2003, *The Colonizer and the Colonized*, London: Earthscan.

Merom, G. 2003, *How Democracies Lose Small Wars: State, Society, and the Failures of France in Algeria, Israel in Lebanon, and the United States in Vietnam*, Cambridge and New York: Cambridge University Press.

Mintz, A. 2001, *Popular Culture and the Shaping of Holocaust Memory in America*, Seattle, WA: University of Washington Press.

Miran, R. 2004, 'Nothing new under the sun', *Haaretz*, 24/09/04.

Monk, D. 2001, *An Aesthetic Occupation: The Immediacy of Architecture and the Palestine Conflict*, Durham, NC: Duke University Press.

Morris, B. 1987, *The Birth of the Palestinian Refugee Problem, 1947–1949*, Cambridge: Cambridge University Press.

Morris, B. 1990, *1948 and After: Israel and the Palestinians*, New York: Oxford University Press.

Morris, B. 1997, *Israel's Border Wars, 1949–1956: Arab Infiltration, Israeli Retaliation, and the Countdown to the Suez War*, New York: Oxford University Press.

Morris, B. 1998, 'Refabricating 1948', *Journal of Palestine Studies*, XXVII, 2.

Moses, A. D. 2004, 'Genocide and Settler Society in Australian History', in Moses, A. D. (ed.), *Genocide and Settler Society: Frontier Violence and Stolen Indigenous Children in Australian History*, New York: Berghahn Books.

Mulvaney, D. J. 1964, 'The Australian Aborigines, 1606–1929; Opinion and Fieldwork', Part 1 and Part 2, in Eastwood, J. J. and Smith, F. B. (eds), *Historical Studies: Selected Articles*, Melbourne: Melbourne University Press.

Murphy, C. 2005, 'Bush's New Book for a New Term', *BBC News*, 21/01/05 <http://news.bbc.co.uk/2/hi/americas/4195303.stm>.

Neumann, K., Thomas, N. and Ericksen, H. (eds) 1999, *Quicksands: Foundational Histories in Australia and Aotearoa New Zealand*, Sydney: University of New South Wales Press.

Nimni, E. 2002, *The Challenge of Post-Zionism: Alternatives to Fundamentalist Politics in Israel*, London: Zed Books.

Oren, A. 2004, 'The defense minister's responsibility', *Haaretz*, 12/05/04.

Oren, A. 2004, 'Rewriting history is easy', *Haaretz*, 01/06/04.

Oren, A. 2005, 'Bro, talk to his brother', *Haaretz*, 01/02/05.

Palestinian Center for Policy and Survey Research 2004, 'Survey Research Unit: Public Opinion Poll #13', 23–26/09/04 <http://www.pcpsr.org/survey/polls/2004/p13a.html>.

Palestinian Center for Policy and Survey Research 2005, 'Survey Research Unit: Public Opinion Poll #15', 10–12/03/05 <http://www.pcpsr.org/survey/polls/2005/p15a.html>.

Pappe, I. 1992, *The Making of the Arab-Israeli Conflict, 1947–51*, London and New York: I. B. Tauris.

Pappe, I. (ed.) 1999, *The Israel/Palestine Question*, London and New York: Routledge.

Pappe, I. 2001, 'Fear, Victimhood, Self and Other', *MIT Electronic Journal of Middle East Studies*, 1.

Pappe, I. 2001, 'The Tantura Case in Israel: The Katz Research and Trial', *Journal of Palestine Studies*, 30, 3.

Pappe, I. 2004, *A History of Modern Palestine: One Land, Two Peoples*, Cambridge: Cambridge University Press.

Pedatzur, R. 2004, 'More than a million bullets', *Haaretz*, 29/06/04.

Pedatzur, R. 2004, 'Pipe dreams', *Haaretz*, 17/10/04.

Philo, G. and Berry, M. 2004, *Bad News From Israel*, London: Pluto Press.

Piterberg, G. 2001, 'Erasures', *New Left Review*, 10.

Porath, Y. 1974, *The Emergence of the Palestinian-Arab National Movement: 1918–1929*, London: Cass.

Program on Negotiation, Harvard Law School 2004, 'Negotiation Conference Examines West Bank and Gaza Settlements', 21/10/04 <http://www.pon.harvard.edu/news/2004/conference_settlers.php3>.

Qumsiyeh, M. B. 2004, *Sharing the Land of Canaan: Human Rights and the Israeli Palestinian Struggle*, London: Pluto Press.

Ram, U. 1999, 'The colonization perspective in Israeli sociology', in Pappe, I. (ed.), *The Israel/Palestine Question*, London and New York: Routledge.

Ram, U. 1995, *The Changing Agenda of Israeli Sociology: Theory, Ideology, and Identity*, Albany, NY: SUNY Press.

Ram, U. 2003, 'There's a time and place for them', *Haaretz*, 14/06/03.

Rapoport, M. 2004, 'Amour, guerre, démographie' *Le Monde Diplomatique*, February issue.

Rapoport, M. 2004, 'A l'ombre du mur, Israël construit des zones industrielles', *Le Monde Diplomatique*, June issue.

Rapoport, M. 2004, 'The Israel election virus', *Haaretz*, 06/12/04.

Rapoport, M. 2005, 'Alone on the barricades', *Haaretz*, 06/05/05.

Rapoport, M. 2005, 'The orange battalion', *Haaretz*, 14/07/05.

Read, P. 2000, *Belonging: Australians, Place and Aboriginal Ownership*, Melbourne: Cambridge University Press.

Reinhart, T. 2003, *Israel/Palestine: How to End the War of 1948*, Sydney: Allen & Unwin.

Reporters Without Borders 2003, *Israel/Palestine: The Black Book*, London: Pluto Press.

Reynolds, H. 1982, *The Other Side of the Frontier: Aboriginal Resistance to the European Invasion of Australia*, Melbourne: Penguin.

Reynolds, H. 1987, *The Law of the Land*, Melbourne: Penguin.

Reynolds, H. 1990, *With the White People*, Melbourne: Penguin.

Reynolds, H. 2001, *An Indelible Stain? The Question of Genocide in Australia's History*, Melbourne: Penguin.

Rivet, D. 2002, *Le Maghreb à l'épreuve de la colonisation*, Paris: Hachette.

Robinson, J. 1995, *The Power of Apartheid: State, Power, and Space in South African Cities*, Oxford and Boston, MA: Butterworth-Heinemann.

Rodinson, M. 1973, *Israel: A Colonial Settler State?*, New York: Monad Press.

Roger, T. 1964, *Modern warfare; a French View of Counterinsurgency*, New York: Praeger.

Rosenblum, D. 2005, 'The chaos is working', *Haaretz*, 21/01/05.

Rosenfeld, A. 2003, *Anti-Americanism and Anti-Semitism: A New Front of Zealotry*, New York: American Jewish Committee.

Ross, D. 2004, *The Missing Peace: The Inside Story of the Fight for Middle East Peace*, New York: Farrar, Straus and Giroux.

Ross, K. 1996, *Fast Cars, Clean Bodies: Decolonisation and the Reordering of French Culture*, Cambridge, MA: MIT Press.

Rowse, T. 2000, 'Indigenous Citizenship' in Hudson, W. and Kane, J. (eds), *Rethinking Australian Citizenship*, Melbourne: Cambridge University Press.

Roy, S. 2001, 'Decline and Disfigurement: The Palestinian Economy after Oslo', in Carey, R. (ed.), *The New Intifada: Resisting Israel's Apartheid*, London: Verso.

Rubin, B. 2004, 'One more Palestinian mistake', *Jerusalem Post*, 12/10/04.

Rubinstein, D. 2005, 'The Battle for the capital', *Haaretz*, 31/03/05.

Rubinstein, D. 2005, 'The Palestinian "crossing"', *Haaretz*, 31/01/05.

Said, E. W. 1994, *Culture and Imperialism*, London: Vintage.

Said, E. W. 2000, 'America's Last Taboo', *New Left Review*, 6.

Said, E. W. 2000, *The End of the Peace Process: Oslo and After*, New York: Pantheon Books.

Said, E. W. 2000, 'Palestinians under Siege', *London Review of Books*, 14/12/00.

Said, E. W. 2001, 'The Only Alternative', *ZNet*, 8/03/01 <http://www.zmag.org/sustainers/content/2001-03/08.said.htm>.

Salpeter, E. 2004, 'The Jewish World/Such a thing as too much support for Israel', *Haaretz*, 05/10/04.

Samet, G. 2004, 'On to the Fifth Republic', *Haaretz*, 31/12/04.

Sarid, Y. 2005, 'Sorry, my stock of pain has run out', *Haaretz*, 24/01/05.

Sartre, J. P. 2001, *Colonialism and Neocolonialism*, London: Routledge.

Sayigh, R. 1994, *Too Many Enemies: The Palestinian Experience in Lebanon*, London: Zed Press.

Segal, Z. 2004, 'Strengthening freedom of speech', *Haaretz*, 07/09/04.

Segev, T. 1986, *1949: The First Israelis*, New York: Free Press.

Segev, T. 1993, *The Seventh Million: The Israelis and the Holocaust*, New York: Hill & Wang.

Segev, T. 2000, *C'était en Palestine au temps des coquelicots*, Paris: Levi.

Shafir, G. 1989, *Land, Labor, and the Origins of the Israeli-Palestinian Conflict, 1882–1914*, Cambridge and New York: Cambridge University Press.

Shafir, G. 1999, 'Zionism and Colonialism: A Comparative Approach', in Pappe, I. (ed.), *The Israel/Palestine Question*, London and New York: Routledge.

Shavit, A. 2003, 'Survival of the fittest? An Interview with Benny Morris', *Haaretz*, 01/09/03.

Shavit, A. 2004, 'The big freeze', *Haaretz*, 08/10/04.

Shavit, A. 2004, 'He took terror to task', *Haaretz*, 15/09/04.

Shavit, A. 2005, 'Chronicle of an end foretold', *Haaretz*, 19/08/05.

Shavit, A. 2005, 'Dividing the Land/Balancing act', *Haaretz*, 08/07/05.

Shavit, A. 2005, 'Parting shots', *Haaretz*, 02/06/05.

Shavit, A. 2005, 'Ready to cross lines', *Haaretz*, 19/07/05.

Shavit, A. 2005, 'Secrets and Lies', *Haaretz*, 19/05/05.

Sheleg, Y. 2004, 'From Durban to The Hague', *Haaretz*, 01/03/04.

Shlaim, A. 1988, *Collusion Across the Jordan: King Abdullah, the Zionist Movement and the Partition of Palestine*, Oxford: Clarendon Press.

Shoat, E. 1992, 'Antinomies of Exile: Said at the Frontier of National Narrations', in Sprinker M. (ed.), *Edward Said: A Critical Reader*, Oxford: Blackwell.

Shohat, O. 2004, 'Throwing the book at Tali Fahima', *Haaretz*, 31/12/04.

Siegman, H. 2003, 'Sharon's Phony War', *New York Review of Books*, 18/12/03.

Silberstein, L. J. 1999, *The Postzionism Debates: Knowledge and Power in Israeli Culture*, New York: Routledge.

Singh, J. 2003, 'The Tel Aviv suicide bombing and illegal foreign workers', *The Electronic Intifada*, 07/01/03 <http://electronicintifada.net/cgi-bin/artman/exec/view.cgi/7/1041>.

Smith, A. D. 1986, 'State-Making and Nation-Building', in Hall, J. A. (ed.), *States in History*, Oxford: Basil Blackwell.

Smith, A. D. 2003, *Chosen Peoples: Sacred Sources of National Identity*, Oxford and New York: Oxford University Press.

Stanner, W. E. H. 1968, *After the Dreaming*, Sydney: Australian Broadcasting Commission.

Stasiulis, D. and Yuval-Davis, N. (eds) 1995, *Unsettling Settler Societies*, London: Sage Publications.

Sternhell, Z. 1998, *The Founding Myths of Israel*, Princeton, NJ: Princeton University Press.

Sternhell, Z. 2005, 'Wanted: a mental revolution', *Haaretz*, 01/07/05.

Suleiman, Y. 2004, *A War of Words: Language and Conflict in the Middle East*, Cambridge: Cambridge University Press.

Tal, A. 2004, 'For the left, Sharon will always be Sharon', *Haaretz*, 26/08/04.

Tal, A. 2004, 'The PLO still sees a single state', *Haaretz*, 14/10/04.

Tarazi, M. 2004, 'Why not two peoples, one state', *New York Times*, 04/10/04.

Thénault, S. 2001, *Une drôle de justice. Les magistrates dans la guerre d'Algérie*, Paris: La Découverte, 2001.

Thompson, L. 1985, *The Political Mythology of Apartheid*, New Haven, CT: Yale University Press.

Thompson, L. 2001, *A History of South Africa*, New Haven, CT: Yale University Press.

Toolis, K. 2003, 'You can't make a deal with the dead', *Guardian*, 10/09/03.

Tutu, D. 2002, 'Apartheid in the Holy Land', *Guardian*, 29/04/02.

van Creveld, M. 1998, *The Sword and the Olive: A Critical History of the Israeli Defense Force*, New York: Public Affairs.

Veracini, L. 2003, 'Of a Contested Ground and an Indelible Stain: The Difficult Reconciliation between Australia and its Aboriginal History during the 1990s and 2000s', *Aboriginal History*, 27.

Veracini, L. (forthcoming), 'Colonialism and Genocides: Towards an Analysis of the Settler Archive of the European Imagination', in Moses, A. D. (ed.), *Genocide and Colonialism*, New York: Berghahn Books.

Veracini, L. (forthcoming), 'The Fourth Geneva Convention and its Relevance for Settler Nations, Including Australia', *Arena Magazine*.

Vidal, D. 1998, *Le Péché originel d'Israel. L'expulsion des Palestiniens revisité par les 'noveaux historiens' israéliens*, Paris: Atélier.

Vittori, J. P. 2000, *On a torturé en Algérie*, Paris: Ramsay.

Wall, I. M. 2002, *France, the United States and the Algerian War*, Berkeley: University of California Press.

Weisberg, J. 2002, *More George W. Bushisms*, New York: Freeside.

Weizman, E. 2003, 'The Geometry of Occupation', *openDemocracy*, 9/09/03, 10/09/03, 15/09/03.

Weizman, E. 2003, 'The Politcs of Verticality', *openDemocracy*, 30/01/03.

Windschuttle, K. 1994, *The Killing of History: How a Discipline is being Murdered by Literary Critics and Social Theorists*, Sydney: Macleay Press.

Windschuttle, K. 2000, 'The Break-Up of Australia', *Quadrant*, September, October, November issues.

Windschuttle, K. 2002, *The Fabrication of Australian History, Vol. 1: Van Dieman's Land, 1803–1847*, Sydney: Macleay Press.

Whitelam, K. W. 1996, *The Invention of Ancient Israel: The Silencing of Palestinian History*, London: Routledge.

Yiftachel, O. 1999, '"Ethnocracy": The politics of Judaising Israel/ Palestine', *Constellations*, 6, 3.

Yiftachel, O. 2002, 'The Shrinking Space of Citizenship: Ethnocratic Politics in Israel', *Middle East Report*, 223 <http://www.merip.org/mer/mer223/223_yiftachel.html>.

Yiftachel, O. 2005, 'Ending the colonialism', *Haaretz*, 19/07/05.

Yovel, J. 2004, 'Security or insecurity?', *Haaretz*, 12/11/04.

Zandberg, E. 2004, 'Surroundings/Watch this space', *Haaretz*, 14/10/04.

Index

Abdullah, King of Jordan 71
Aboriginal history 74–8
Aboriginal reconciliation 67, 77,
  81, 84, 96, 128 n55
Adalah, Center for the Protection
  of Israeli Arabs' Legal Rights
  107 n47
Afrikaner nationalism 18, 19, 20,
  23
Against Paranoid Nationalism 66
Agamben, Giorgio 12
Agha, Hussein 53
American Israel Public Affairs
  Committee (AIPAC) 89, 90,
  131 n13
Algeria 41–2, 45, 48, 53, 55,
  60–1, 108 n55, 109 n3, 110 n6,
  115 n40, 116 n44, 120 n70,
  120 n72
Algerian war of decolonization 14,
  43, 45, 47, 52, 53, 54–5, 56,
  59, 60, 108 n55, 109 n3, 111
  n7, 112 n16, 115 n31, 115 n36,
  115 n40, 116 n43, 116 n44,
  120 n70
Aliyas, Jewish migration to
  Palestine 21
American Jewish Committee 129
  n7
ANC, African National Congress
  17, 23
Anglican Church 101 n2
Anti-Semitism 89, 130 n7
Apartheid 16–18, 19, 20, 23, 25,
  27, 29–30, 31–2, 33–4, 37, 40,
  60, 101 n5
Apartheid legislation 30, 38, 105
  n39
Arabic language 28

Arafat, Yasser 7, 9, 56
Armée de Libération Nationale
  (Algeria) 54
Aron, Raymond 110 n6
Assimilation 62, 86
Association 62
Attwood, Bain 76, 84
Aussaresses, French general 116
  n44
Australia 64–6, 67, 74–8, 78–9,
  82, 83, 84, 87, 120 n3, 125
  n40, 127 n48, 127 n49, 128
  n55
The Australian Women's Weekly
  127 n48

Bakri, Mohammed 61, 119 n64
Balfour Declaration 98 n7
Balibar, Etienne 13
Bantustans 25, 26, 27, 30, 32
Bantustanization 11, 27, 28, 32,
  33, 94, 96
Barak, Ehud 7, 8, 27, 132 n24
Bassi, Yonatan 134 n33
La battaglia di Algieri 61
Battle of Algiers 61, 116 n44
Begin–Sadat Center for Strategic
  Studies, Bar-Ilan University 108
  n63
Ben Cramer, Richard 112 n18
Benvenisti, Meron 29, 32, 94, 101
  n5
Benn, Aluf 56, 105 n37
Benziman, Uzi 107 n51
Bernstein, Tom 130 n11
Berque, Jacques 63
Betselem 109 n67
Betts, Raymond 62
Bi-national State 94–5

Black South Africans 17, 19, 23,
    27, 30, 38
Boim, Zeev 36
Bophutatswana 25
Breaking the Silence 10
Bringing Them Home Report 67
British Association of University
    Teachers 101 n2
British Empire 61
Bush, George W 89, 90, 90, 130
    n10, 130 n11

Camp David summit 8, 24, 62,
    64, 134 n34
Carr, Bob 121 n3
Casbahs 91
The Case for Democracy 89, 130
    n11
Center for Political Research 16
Challe, French general 53
Citizenship Law (Israel) 30, 101
    n5, 106 n46, 107 n47
Claiming a Continent 127 n48
Clark, Helen 127 n48
Clayton, Anthony 53, 55, 115
    n40, 116 n43
Clinton, Bill 24, 88, 92
Cold War 18, 24, 43, 45, 87
Colonialism 1–3, 6, 33, 58, 63,
    92, 93, 96, 98 n5, 100 n32, 133
    n24, 133 n31
The Colonizer and the Colonized 4
Colons 60–1
Conklin, Alice 62
Conquest of labour 21
Counter-insurgency 12, 43, 51,
    52, 53–4, 55, 115 n40, 116 n44
Culture and Imperialism 58, 59

D'Alema, Massimo 25
Day, David 127 n48
Decolonization 6, 8, 11, 12, 14,
    31, 43, 44, 45, 47, 60, 61–3,
    80, 93, 95–6, 120 n69, 121 n7,
    133 n32

Defense Shield, operation 35, 53,
    54
De Gaulle, Charles 42, 47, 57, 63,
    96, 110 n5, 120 n70
Deir Yassin effect 70
de Klerk, Frederick 18, 96
Denoon, Donald 84
Dershowitz, Alan Morton 131
    n16
Desert (Bedouin) Reconnaissance
    Battalion 46, 111 n15
Dien Bien Phu 63
Disengagement 5, 7, 26–7, 29, 33,
    35, 42, 46, 48, 50, 51, 59, 63,
    82, 94, 96, 101 n5, 105 n37,
    108 n58, 112 n21, 118 n59
Druze servicemen in the Israeli
    Army 46, 111 n15

East Jerusalem 24, 28, 29, 37, 39,
    42
Eban, Abba 5, 6
The Economist 17, 18
Eldar, Akiva 25
*The Emergence of the Palestinian-
    Arab National Movement* 69
Erez 35, 36
Evacuation 26, 48, 49, 50, 94–5,
    110 n6, 112 n21, 113 n27, 114
    n29, 134 n33
Evengelical (Zionist) Christians
    13, 131 n14
Evans, Ray 122 n10
Evian negotiations 60

Fahima, Tali 8–9
Fanon, Frantz 6, 11–12, 60, 100
    n29, 100 n32, 108 n55, 120 n2,
    133 n31
Farsakh, Leila 20, 22, 24, 104 n29
Fieldhouse, David 1
Fifth French Republic 43, 47, 111
    n8
Finkelstein, Norman 102 n8
The Founding Myths of Israel 72

Fourth French Republic 47, 63
Fourth Geneva Convention 121
    n7
France 6, 41, 43, 44–5, 46, 47, 48,
    49, 61, 93, 95, 109 n3, 110 n6,
    115 n40, 120 n70
Franklin 'affair' 90
Frontierity 19, 102 n12
Front de Libération Nationale
    (FLN) 44, 45, 57, 109 n3

Gaza 3–5, 10, 14, 24, 27, 29, 35,
    36, 39, 46, 48, 50, 52, 114n 29,
    117 n51, 120 n72
Green Line 22, 30, 32, 95, 96,
    109 n69
Gregory, Derek 37
Guardian 57

Haaretz 3, 15, 25, 51, 52, 56, 57,
    58, 90, 100 n22, 101 n5, 105
    n37, 116 n41, 117 n51, 130
    n11, 131 n12, 133 n24
Hage, Ghassan 66, 83
Hajjar, Lisa 12, 115 n36
Halper, Jeff 32, 37, 93, 113 n25
Hamas 4, 5
Hanafi, Sari 133 n32
Harkis, Algerian military
    personnel serving in the French
    army 46
Harward Law School 114 n29
Hass, Amira 39
Hebron 114 n28
Herziliya conference (2004) 106
    n41
Herzl, Theodor 98 n5
High Court of Australia 76
History wars 66
Homelands 25, 101 n5
Holbrooke, Richard 89
Howard, John 82, 127 n49
Human Rights and Equal
    Opportunity Commission
    (Australia) 67

il manifesto 15
Indigenocide 122 n10
Indochina (Vietnam) 45, 56, 115
    n40
International Court of Justice 16,
    121 n7
Intifada 2, 5, 10, 11, 14, 31, 34,
    35, 38, 39, 45, 51, 53, 54, 55,
    56, 59, 60, 62, 94
Israeli Committee Against House
    Demolitions 107 n51
Israeli Defense Force (IDF) 3, 10,
    46, 48, 52, 53, 61, 111 n15,
    112 n21, 113 n22, 113 n23,
    115 n37, 117 n51, 118 n55
Israeli Defense Force Archive 118
    n56

Jabarin, Hasan 107 n47
Jenin 8, 9, 61
Jenin Jenin 61
Jericho 89
Jerusalem 42, 106 n41
Jerusalem Post 41, 94
Jewsweek 90
Jubran, Karim 109 n67
Judt, Tony 110 n6

Karin A 45
Katz, Teddy 118 n55
Keating, Paul 96
Keinon, Herb 41
Kerry, John 89
Kimmerling, Baruch 2, 102 n12,
    122 n10
Kissinger, Henry 134 n34
Krauthammer, Charles 55–6

Labour policies 20–2, 34, 35–6,
    120 n72
*Land, Labor, and the Origins of
    the Israeli-Palestinian Conflict* 2
Laor, Yitzhak 36, 38
The Law of the Land 76
Law of Return (Israel) 31

Lebanon 45, 56, 115 n40, 119 n60
Levy, Daniel 7
Levy, Gideon 100 n22, 113 n23
Lieberman, Avigdor 106 n41
Likud Party 46
Little, Douglas 129 n6
Low, Donald Anthony 61
Lukacs, Georg 11–12, 60

Maariv 34, 115 n37
Mabo, Eddie 76
Mabo judgment of the High Court
    of Australia 76, 79, 80, 81, 84
Malley, Robert 53
Mandela, Nelson 17
Manifesto of the 121 47
Mapai 68
Marcus, Yoel 3–5, 98 n9, 110, n5
Masalha, Nur 123 n22
Matrix of control 32, 107 n51
Memmi, Albert 4, 99 n10, 99 n14
Military Intelligence (Israel) 52
Mobility restriction 33, 37–8, 109
    n67
Morice Line 46
Morris, Benny 70, 123 n18, 127
    n51

Nakba, the expulsion of
    Palestinians that accompanied
    the establishment of Israel 18,
    123 n19
Narrative, memory, remembrance
    2, 7, 8, 51, 57–61, 64, 69, 76,
    78, 83, 84, 87, 90, 91, 123,
    n19, 125 n37, 129 n7, 130 n7
Nasser, Abdel 46
National Geographic 66, 91
National Museum of Australia 77
National Union Party 106 n41
Neo-Zionism 20
Netanyahu, Binyamin 41, 82, 117
    n51
New York Review of Books 53
New York Times 94

Occupation 22, 27, 32, 42, 47, 50,
    52, 84, 90, 101 n2, 105 n37,
    107 n53, 112 n18, 113 n23,
    115 n40, 120 n72, 132 n18
Occupied Palestinian Territories
    11, 14, 21, 24, 25, 27, 31, 33,
    32, 34, 35, 37, 38, 39, 43, 48,
    54, 55, 61, 62, 86, 88, 91, 92,
    96, 108 n55, 114 n29, 115 n40,
    116 n43, 132 n18
Old Testament 91
Or Commission 28
Oren, Amir 57, 130 n11
Organisation Armée Secrète
    (OAS) 49, 61
Oslo Accords 3, 5, 26, 33, 38, 79,
    81, 85, 86, 103 n15
Oslo arrangements 27, 31, 33,
    102 n8, 105 n37
Oslo, peace process 8, 23, 24, 34,
    61, 64, 67, 80, 88, 94, 104 n29,
    125 n37, 131 n16
Oslo, period of 23, 27, 35, 38, 51,
    52, 59, 108 n55
The Other Side of the Frontier 75

Palestine Liberation Organization
    (PLO) 44, 85, 94
Palestinian Authority 4, 5, 27, 28,
    29, 35, 39, 46, 133 n24
Palestinian Diaspora and Refugee
    Center 133 n32
Palestinian Israelis 17, 22, 23, 27,
    28, 30, 31, 65, 81, 83, 96, 104
    n25, 106 n41
Palestinians of the Occupied
    Territories 22, 28, 30, 32, 37,
    39, 65, 83, 96, 104 n25, 133
    n25, 134 n33
Pappe, Ilan 102 n11, 118 n55
Pedatzur, Reuven 116 n41
Pfimlin, Pierre 63
Politicide 122 n10
Pontecorvo, Gillo 61
Porath, Yehoshua 69

Post-Zionism 47, 128 n51
Powell, Colin 5, 90
Public letter of Israeli Air Force
    pilots 47, 112 n20

Quadrant 125 n40
Qulandiyah checkpoint 39–40
Qassam rockets 3, 4, 59

Rabin, Yitzhak 9
Racialization 36–7, 108 n63
Rafah 111 n15, 121 n3
Rapoport, Meron 36, 120 n70
Ravitz, Avraham 133 n31
Read, Peter 85
*Rebel Hearts Journeys Within the
    IRA's Soul* 57
Reciprocity 9, 59
Redfern 121 n3
Reinhart, Tanya 105 n38
Reynolds, Henry 75, 76, 125 n40
Rhodes, Cecil 22
Rhodesian option 49, 114 n28
Rice, Condoleeza 89, 90, 130 n11,
    131 n12
Riposte, military doctrine of
    counter-insurgency 116 n43
Road Map 26, 31, 131 n12
Robertson, Pat 13
Rodinson Maxime 97 n4
Rosenblum, Doron 119 n69
Ross, Dennis 64,
Ross, Kristin 44
Rothschild family 98 n5
Rubin, Barry 94
Rubinstein, Danny 58
Ruddock, Philip 77
Rusk, Dean 62

Sadat, Anwar 58
Sahara 61
Said, Edward 11, 16, 17, 24, 31,
    58, 59, 60, 100 n29, 129 n4,
    132 n20
Salazar regime (Portugal) 63
Salpeter, Eliahu 90

Samet, Gideon 111 n8
Sarid, Yossi 114 n28
Sartre, Jean-Paul 6, 47, 48, 99
    n13, 99 n14, 112 n17
Segev, Tom 71
Segregation 11, 17, 27, 28, 31, 37,
    38, 39, 79, 109 n67
Separation barrier (fence,
    apartheid wall) 11, 17, 27, 28,
    30, 31, 32, 34, 35, 37, 38, 39,
    46, 79, 94, 95, 101 n5, 109
    n67, 121 n7
September 11 92, 130 n10, 132
    n16
Settler imagination 19, 68, 88
Settler mentality 85
Settler society 1–2, 50, 73, 78, 82,
    83, 91, 92, 96
Settler state, polity 2, 6, 32, 80,
    82, 83, 97 n4, 114 n28
The Seventh Million 71
Shafir, Gershon 78
Shapira, Anita 2
Sharansky, Nathan 89, 130 n11
Sharon, Ariel 7, 25, 26, 27, 28,
    29, 35, 42, 43, 45, 47, 49, 54,
    56, 63, 81, 110 n5, 112 n22,
    117 n51, 131 n12
Shavit, Ari 105 n37
Shin Bet 52, 55, 100 n22, 106 n46
Shlaim, Avi 71
Shoat, Ella 132 n20
Silberstein, Laurence 31
Smith, Anthony 2, 19, 24, 97 n3
South Africa 17, 18, 19, 20, 21,
    22, 23, 24, 25, 27, 28, 29, 32,
    34, 40, 95, 101 n5, 103 n14,
    104 n29
South African National Party 18
Stanner, William Edward Hanley
    74
Sternhell, Zeev 9, 72, 73, 95, 103
    n19

Tantura 118 n55
Tarazi, Michael 94

Tel Aviv 25, 34
Terra nullius, legal doctrine 76, 81
'Territories, Live' 132 n18
Toolis, Kevin 57
Transfer (of indigenous
    populations) 19, 20, 22, 28, 33,
    44, 103 n15, 123 n22
Tutu, Desmond 40

Unilateralism 25, 27, 32, 33, 35,
    55, 59, 62, 73, 85, 94, 96, 119
    n69
United Nations General Assembly
    121 n7
United States 24, 53, 90, 91, 92,
    121 n7, 131 n16, 132 n20
US Global Anti-Semitism
    Awareness Act 89
US opinion, constituencies,
    perceptions 17, 87, 88, 89, 90,
    91, 104 n30, 117 n44, 129 n2,
    129 n3, 131 n14, 132 n19
US Middle East policy 24, 43, 88,
    91, 92, 129 n6
US suburbia 88

War on Terror 24, 45
Washington Post 55
Weisglass, Dov 105 n37, 131 n12
Weizman, Eyal 107 n53

West Bank 14, 17, 21, 23, 24, 27,
    31, 32, 33, 34, 35, 37, 38, 42,
    43, 44, 46, 48, 53, 54, 55, 91,
    92, 93, 114 n28, 114 n29, 134
    n34
Whitlam, Gough 122 n14
Windschuttle, Keith 77, 81, 122
    n12, 125 n40, 127 n51
World Conference Against Racism
    16
World Council of Churches 101 n2
The Wretched of the Earth 11, 59

Yaalon, Moshe 36, 51, 112 n21,
    112 n22, 115 n33
Yedioth Ahronoth 10, 111 n6
Yiftachel, Oren 106 n43, 133 n24
Yitzhaki, Aryeh 114 n28
Yushuv 71, 72

Zeevi, Rehavam 9
Zionism 2, 10, 11, 14, 19, 20, 21,
    22, 24, 31, 65, 66, 68, 69, 71,
    72, 73, 82, 86, 98 n5, 102 n12,
    103 n15, 103 n19, 124 n28
Zionism and Territory 2
Zionist left 29, 43, 47, 69, 124
    n28
Zionist lobby in the US 24, 88
    129 n4